Total Responsibility Management
The Manual

Sandra Waddock and Charles Bodwell

Cases by Jennifer Leigh

Sandra Waddock is Professor of Management at Boston College's Carroll School of Management and Senior Research Fellow at BC's Center for Corporate Citizenship. She holds the MBA and DBA degrees from Boston University and has published over 100 articles on corporate responsibility, corporate citizenship and inter-sector collaboration in journals such as *The Academy of Management Journal*, *Academy of Management Executive*, *Strategic Management Journal*, *The Journal of Corporate Citizenship*, *Human Relations* and *Business and Society*. Author of *Leading Corporate Citizens* (McGraw-Hill, 2nd edn 2006), co-editor of *Unfolding Stakeholder Thinking* (Greenleaf Publishing, 2002, 2003), and *Learning to Talk* (Greenleaf Publishing, 2004), she is a founding faculty of the Leadership for Change Program, co-founder (with Stephen Lydenberg and Brad Googins) of the Institute for Responsible Investing, initiated Business Ethics' 100 Best Corporate Citizens ranking with co-author Samuel Graves and editor Marjorie Kelly, and edited *The Journal of Corporate Citizenship* from 2003 to 2004. She received the 2004 Sumner Marcus Award for Distinguished Service from the Social Issues in Management Division of the Academy of Management, and the 2005 Faculty Pioneer Award for External Impact by the Aspen Institute Business in Society Program and the World Resources Institute. She has been a visiting scholar at the Harvard Kennedy School of Government (2006–2007) and University of Virginia Darden Graduate School of Business (2000).

Charles Bodwell is currently the manager of the ILO's Factory Improvement Programme (FIP), a Swiss- and US-funded project linking competitiveness with improved labour practices. As with TRM, FIP takes a holistic view of organisations, focusing on establishing strengthened systems, improved measurement, broad-based involvement and a commitment to continuous improvement. With FIP, Charles is currently working with auto and motorcycle parts supplier factories in India and garment factories in Vietnam and Sri Lanka (see more on FIP at www.ilofip.org). Prior to taking over FIP, as a senior specialist in the International Labour Office his work focused on corporate citizenship and supply chain issues, in particular the CSR efforts of large multinational enterprises. It was while based at ILO headquarters in Geneva that he developed, together with Sandra Waddock, the TRM model as well as the FIP approach to upgrading production facilities. He has been a graduate researcher at Cambridge University, visiting professor at the Helsinki School of Economics and visiting scholar at Stanford University. He has worked for IBM, Agfa and Schlumberger, while also consulting to various *Fortune* 500 companies. He has an MBA from McGill University and a Master's of International Management from ESADE. He currently lives in Bangkok, Thailand, with his wife Ivanka and three sons, Tomi, Matija and Nikola.

Total Responsibility Management

The Manual

Sandra Waddock and Charles Bodwell

Cases by Jennifer Leigh

Greenleaf
PUBLISHING
2 0 0 7

© 2007 Greenleaf Publishing Ltd

Published by Greenleaf Publishing Limited
Aizlewood's Mill
Nursery Street
Sheffield S3 8GG
UK
www.greenleaf-publishing.com

Printed on environmentally friendly, acid-free paper from managed forests
by CPI Antony Rowe, Chippenham and Eastbourne
Cover by LaliAbril.com.

British Library Cataloguing in Publication Data:
   Waddock, Sandra A.
      Total responsibility management : the manual
      1. Social responsibility of business
      I. Title II. Bodwell, Charles
      658.4'08

ISBN 978-1-874719-98-4

Contents

Acknowledgements

This manual is based on research into the theory of Total Responsibility Management conducted in co-operation with and support from a variety of colleagues, including Ivanka Mamic, Nikolai Rogovsky and Arturo Tolentino at the International Labour Office.

The cases were written by Jennifer Leigh, Gettysburg College, in co-operation with Boston College and the International Labour Office, Geneva, Switzerland, in 2001–2002, updated from company websites, and are based primarily on interviews with CSR participants in study companies.

Publication of this work, including case studies, does not constitute endorsement by the ILO or Boston College.

List of boxes, figures and tables

1

What is responsibility management? And why bother?

Almost every manager today knows that satisfying customers by meeting their quality demands is a critical component of business success. Quality management is a given in modern companies, a competitive imperative. Yet it was not always so. Back when the quality movement was getting started, few managers really understood either the importance of quality to customers or how to manage for quality. Much the same could be said today about managing responsibility as was said about the early days of quality management. Why should responsibility be managed? What is responsibility management? Who cares? And, importantly, *how* can responsibility be managed? This manual will attempt to answer these questions and provide a *framework* for managing a company's responsibilities to stakeholders and the natural environment that can be applied in a wide range of contexts.

Perhaps the analogy to the quality movement will help. Companies know that product or service quality affects their customer relationships and the trust customers have in the company's products and services. So too a company's management of its responsibilities to other constituencies affects its relationships with those other stakeholders and the natural environment. But why bother? The answer is quite simple. Never has it been easier for employees, reporters, activists, non-governmental organisations (NGOs), community members, the media and other critical observers to find fault with companies and their subsidiaries. A problem identified, even in a remote region or within a remote supplier, can virtually instantaneously be transmitted around the world at the click of a mouse. Ask footwear, toy and clothing and other highly visible branded companies what their recent experience with corporate critics has been and they will tell you about the need to manage their stakeholder (i.e. human rights, labour relations, environmental, integrity-related) responsibilities or face significant consequences in the limelight of public opinion.

Even companies without brand names experience increasing pressures to manage responsibility from social investors, employees and their customers in the supply chains they serve. *Stakeholders*, those who are affected by or can affect the company's activities,[1] *care* about how a company treats them, about impacts companies have on others, on society, on themselves. Increasingly, employees, customers, investors, environmental activists, the media, suppliers, communities and governments and others are making their concerns known in visible ways. Complicating matters further, many companies today find that outsiders seldom make distinctions between the company doing the sourcing and members of its supply and distribution chains. Critics of companies seem to believe that the sourcing company can and should be held responsible for whatever happens throughout their supply and distribution chains. Companies doing the sourcing are forced to respond to these concerns because otherwise their reputation—and business—suffers.

No company can hope to avoid criticism entirely, of course, because all companies have impacts on stakeholders and the natural environment; some of these impacts will undoubtedly create concerns among some stakeholders. However efficiently a company operates, problems can

---

1   The classic definition of a stakeholder, given here, comes from Freeman 1984.

arise, particularly if the company mindlessly barges ahead with decisions that affect employees, communities, suppliers, customers and activists concerned about the natural environment—without consulting with them. What companies *can* do is to manage their stakeholder-related responsibilities in ways that minimise negative impacts, build trust and thereby reduce potential criticism. In short, they can manage the *relationships* that they build with stakeholders (and activists concerned with nature) and the practices that the company uses to produce and deliver goods and services. It is this process of managing relationships and company impacts that responsibility management is all about.

Responsibility management occurs through a systemic process that in other writing we have called 'total responsibility management' or TRM—to make an analogy with already-familiar processes of management quality, total quality management, TQM (see, for example, Waddock and Bodwell 2002; see also Waddock and Bodwell 2004). Further, whether you do it consciously or not, you are *already* managing responsibility, just as companies were already managing quality when the quality movement hit. Sometimes they were just doing it badly or mindlessly!

In reality, companies manage their responsibilities to stakeholders and the natural environment through the operating practices and strategies they evolve to accomplish their goals. They do so because responsibilities are integral when there are impacts—and few managerial decisions have no impacts on either one group of stakeholders or another or on the natural environment. Just think of the array of corporate functions with the term 'relations' in typical titles: employee and labour relations, supplier relations, community relations, investor relations, customer relations, government relations, and the list goes on. This manual will make that process of managing responsibilities to and relationships with stakeholders and nature more explicit. Making the process explicit is important because too few of today's decision-makers yet understand how they are managing stakeholder responsibilities as well as they understand how to manage quality.

1.1 What is responsibility management?

Managing responsibilities goes well beyond traditional 'do good' or discretionary activities associated with philanthropy and volunteerism, which are frequently termed 'corporate social responsibility' and sometimes associated with narrow definitions of corporate citizenship. In its broadest sense, responsibility management means taking corporate citizenship seriously as a core part of the way the company develops and implements its business model. In this broad sense, responsibility management focuses on managing *corporate responsibilities*, which involves managing stakeholder relationships and the companies' impacts on stakeholders. It thus focuses on the nature and impacts of company practices with respect to all important stakeholders and the natural environment.

From this perspective, managing responsibility means building trusting relationships with key stakeholders, such as employees, customers, suppliers and communities, and ensuring that, despite power differences that may exist, the company's impacts are positive rather than negative. Managing responsibility therefore means working to reduce the negative impacts of corporate activities and developing mutually beneficial practices and ways of interacting (or engaging) with stakeholders so that long-term relationships can develop. It can mean active engagement with critics of the company as well as governments, to gain their perspectives and inputs, as well as with those primary stakeholders on whom the company's existence depends: investors, employees, customers and suppliers/distributors. Increasingly, it also means using natural resources in ways that are sustainable over the long term, as the European Union's white paper on corporate social responsibility makes clear. The specifics of responsibility management are unique to each company, its industry, its products and its stakeholders, yet, as this manual illustrates, a general approach to managing responsibility is feasible—indeed, is increasingly necessary.

Relationships with key stakeholders (including stakeholders such as trade unions, employee associations and NGOs, who might be critical of the company) enable companies to problem-solve *with* stakeholders from a basis of trust rather than a more adversarial base. With explicit responsibility management systems in place, company leaders can work problems out *with* stakeholders, rather than allowing those problems to fester and ultimately damage the company and its reputation, not to mention its stakeholders or the natural environment. Responsibility management can be quite complex; however, the general framework for responsibility management is very similar to other management systems with which managers are already familiar, including quality and environmental management systems. Let us focus on the comparison with quality management, as quality approaches are best known.

Managing for quality fundamentally means paying attention to what customers actually need and want, rather than assuming that the company knows best, and working to deliver on those needs and wants. Managing responsibility similarly means paying attention to the needs and interests of stakeholders in much the same way, but of a significantly broader array of increasingly vocal stakeholders. Employees, customers, suppliers and distributors, other allies and partners, communities where the company locates facilities (or where the supply chain members are located), owners and investors, creditors, and local, regional and national governments are among the stakeholders to whom it makes sense to pay attention.

Yes, paying attention to the interests and concerns of all of these stakeholders can be difficult and adds significantly to the complexity of the manager's job. Yes, it is probably infeasible to meet the demands of all of them—and no one expects that any company will do that. But numerous companies have discovered to their chagrin the costs of ignoring serious or significant stakeholder interests and concerns and have had their reputations tarnished as a result. Think, for example, of the accusations against Nike of sweatshop labour practices in its supply chain, the reputational damage to Liz Claiborne over the same accusations, or the challenges Shell faced in its dealings with Greenpeace over the decommissioning of the Brent Spar drilling platform. More recently, consider the impact of lack of consideration of customer needs and concerns with Merck's belated withdrawal of Vioxx after concerns about heart problems were known.

In contrast, think about the forward-looking publication of a transparent report about real problems—and what is being done about them in a similar situation by The Gap in 2004.[2] The result of a lack of such attention can be lost customers, difficulty recruiting talent or problems with locating in certain communities, for example. Although it is not easy identifying significant problems that exist internally, the demands on companies to be more transparent and to use their power more wisely are intensifying. Through forward-looking disclosure and active engagement with stakeholders, all elements of responsibility management, companies can avoid tarnished reputations and potentially more serious restrictions on their activities.

Awareness of the concerns and interests of stakeholders, both inside and outside the company, can only enhance company performance and decision-making processes, especially since companies cannot do business today without encountering these groups in some way. Thus, whether they do it explicitly or not, whether they do it well or not, companies *are* managing responsibilities. The key to making responsibility management part of the company's business success is to make explicit and discussable in a variety of forums the stakeholders' interests and concerns, and work jointly and collaboratively at times, and within the company at other times, to ensure that these concerns do not become significant problems.

1.2 How to manage responsibility

Using the TRM framework is not rocket science. As we pointed out above, companies are already managing their responsibilities to stakeholders. It simply needs to be done using the same management techniques, problem-solving techniques, engagement strategies and systemic strategies already in use for managing quality. Similar thought processes and techniques can be applied to the relationships with other stakeholders beyond customers and employees, who are the focus of quality. TRM is

2   The Gap's forward-looking and highly transparent social report can be found along with more recent reports at www.gapinc.com/public/ SocialResponsibility/sr_report.shtml (accessed December 2006).

simply a systemic *framework* for managing responsibility for all of the companies' stakeholder- and natural environment-related activities: that is, a system of *total responsibility management*. By making responsibility management explicit, TRM has the capacity to help companies develop integrity, values-driven vision, and respect for the perspectives of stakeholders affected by the company's business activities.

Briefly, TRM starts with *inspiration*. Inspiration means that the company has articulated a values-driven vision to which top management is committed. This vision provides inspiration because it creates meaning for stakeholders engaged in a range of processes, partnerships and other relationships with the business. Built on generally agreed foundational standards that provide a *floor* of expectations about company practices and performance while incorporating the company's own explicitly stated values, the vision guides strategy development and implementation, processes, procedures and relationships.

The next major component of TRM is *integration*. TRM *integrates* the company's inspirational vision into its strategies, its employee relationships and practices, and the numerous management systems that support company strategies. Each company needs to determine how to do this in a way that satisfies its particular stakeholders, industry demands and product array.

TRM, using continual improvement tools creates feedback loops that foster *innovation and improvement* in management systems. Innovations and improvements in various strategies and stakeholder-related operating practices can potentially boost performance, and improve results. Key performance *indicators*, or a measurement system that assesses how well the company is performing along at least the triple bottom line of economic, social and environment (Elkington 1998) is an important element of the TRM framework, as are transparency and accountability for results. Box 1.1 provides an overview of the elements of the TRM framework, which is also pictured (for the more visually minded) in Figure 1.1. Each of these elements will be dealt with in greater detail in the following chapters, following a brief exploration of the 'business case' for responsibility management.

TRM IN BRIEF

INSPIRATION: VISION SETTING AND LEADERSHIP SYSTEMS

1. **Responsibility vision, values and leadership commitments**. Each firm determines its own vision for responsible practice and leadership, based on a foundation of generally agreed global standards and values as articulated by international bodies. The company makes a commitment to responsibility management through the top-management team and leaders throughout the organisation. This commitment helps the company determine not only 'What business are we in?' and 'How do we compete?' but also 'What do we stand for?' in developing its responsibility vision, enhancing leadership commitments and implementing core values that underpin all of its activities

2. **Stakeholder engagement processes**. Stakeholder engagement means developing dialogue, communication and mutuality with important stakeholders to inform operating practices and strategies. The company determines 'What is our impact on stakeholders?' and 'How do we appropriately incorporate the views of key stakeholders into our responsibility vision and leadership?' through its stakeholder engagement processes. Stakeholders include: primary stakeholders (employees, unions, owners, supplier/allies and customers) and critical secondary stakeholders (communities and governments). Specific other stakeholders may also be included, depending on the company's situation and industry

INTEGRATION: STRATEGY, EMPLOYEE AND OPERATING PRACTICES

3. **Strategy**. Having determined its responsibility vision and stakeholder engagement strategy, a company then develops an overall strategy for achieving its vision, leadership and corporate goals in a responsible way. The company asks, 'How do we match our vision and what we stand for with the reality of what we do and are?' and 'How do we achieve our corporate goals and

Box 1.1 TRM in brief (continued opposite)

objectives consistent with our inspirational vision and core values?'

4. **Human resource responsibility**. It is people who are organised in organisations. It is people who implement the company's vision and leadership and particularly determine how responsibly the company operates. People involved with a company, whether directly as employees or in the supply chain for a company, deserve to be treated responsibly: that is, with dignity and respect. Responsibility for human resource practices thus stretches beyond a company's formal boundaries to include other companies taking part in a focal company's value chain. Responsibility for human resources includes key elements of training, performance appraisal, recruitment, retention, and dismissal policies, wage and salary policies consistent with local conditions, working conditions, and employee development, communication and empowerment practices, including union relationships and commitment to meeting (at minimum) internationally agreed labour standards

5. **Responsibility integration management systems**. Responsibility is integral to corporate practices, impacts and relationships. This integration means that corporate practices and relations are either responsible or they are not. Recognising this reality, TRM companies develop management systems that explicitly and deliberately integrate an understanding and implementation of responsibility into all management systems as well as corporate strategies. Key systems include reward systems, information and communication systems, operating, production and delivery systems, purchasing, accounting and financial systems, environmental systems, marketing and sales systems, human resource systems, and other corporate systems, supplier/ally relationships, and others as relevant

INNOVATION: IMPROVEMENT AND LEARNING SYSTEMS

6. **Improvement: remediation, innovation and learning**. Implementing a responsibility vision is an ongoing, cyclical

Box 1.1 (from previous page; continued over)

process of continual remediation for wrongs, improvement, innovation and organisational learning. Data from the measurement and accountability systems provides managers with guidance and structures that encourage responsible practices and provide an emphasis on continued organisational learning and development towards ever–more responsible practice. Remediation links to both the foundational values agreed by the international community and the specific responsibility vision of the corporation, focusing on continually learning and improving practices that are generally responsible but could be performed better, while immediately eliminating practices that are intolerable under the foundational values. The stakeholder dialogue process also provides key data for process, standards and system improvements

. . . PLUS INDICATORS TO FEED BACK INTO THE IMPROVEMENT AND INNOVATION SYSTEM

7. **Responsibility measurement system.** Measurement of the impacts and responsibility of both the processes and results of systems and corporate practices in a multiple (at least triple, i.e. economic, social and ecological)–bottom–line framework is a critical component of implementing and understanding a responsibility vision. Responsible companies know that their stakeholder impacts can and need to be measured regularly and consistently so that results can be reported both internally and externally and improvements can be made where necessary. Measurement systems evaluate stakeholder impacts and performance through strategic and functional area assessments. Data gathered through measurement procedures, information technology systems, and responsibility auditing practices provide a baseline for continually improving operating practices, highlighting urgent situations, providing feedback on progress, and fostering accountability to internal and external stakeholders through valid and reliable assessment/auditing practices

Box 1.1 (from previous page; continued opposite)

8. **Results: responsible economic performance, stakeholder/societal and ecological outcomes**. The outcomes of productive processes in a company are its results—and the consequent impacts on stakeholders and the natural environment. The responsibility measurement systems help a company assess its performance multi-dimensionally and with a multiple-bottom-line orientation that permits comprehensive performance assessment along traditional financial as well as stakeholder and ecological lines

9. **Transparency and accountability for results and impacts**. The responsible company knows that it needs to be accountable for its stakeholder and ecological impacts and results, and also to report those impacts and its operating results transparently through at least a triple-bottom-line framework (economic, societal and ecological). Data from the responsibility measurement system are used to produce responsibility reports addressing internal and external practices and the impacts of corporate activities. Companies determine how to develop trust with external and internal stakeholders through dialogue and assure the validity and reliability of their accountability systems in a cost-effective way

Box 1.1 (from previous page)

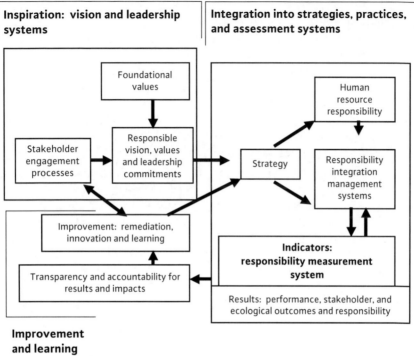

| Inspiration: vision and leadership systems | Integration into strategies, practices, and assessment systems |

Improvement and learning systems

FIGURE 1.1 The total responsibility management system

1.3 Managing quality . . . managing responsibility

As noted above, responsibility management has much in common with quality or environmental management, both of which have become familiar managerial practices in recent years. Responsibility management is a *process* or a system involving development of vision, explicit articulation of values, implementation into strategies and management systems and continual improvements. To be effective, responsibility management requires commitment from top management, commitment that recognises the importance of managing responsibility to achieving the company's long-term objectives, building positive relationships with important stakeholders and generating positive returns. In all of these elements, TRM resembles TQM in more than superficial ways, some of which are briefly explored below.

Companies 'managed' quality for years without realising they were doing so. The result was, in the eyes of many customers, poor quality. Only when quality management became explicit through the quality movement of the 1980s and 1990s, which evolved from Japanese and German implementation of quality management processes developed by people such as W. Edwards Deming and Joseph Juran, among others, in earlier decades, did quality begin to improve significantly. Similarly, the reality is that some degree of responsibility—or irresponsibility—*is already present* in all of a company's stakeholder-related practices, activities and relationships whether it manages it effectively or not, just as some degree of quality (or lack thereof) was present in products and services before quality was explicitly managed.

Continuing the analogy with quality management, TRM follows the traditional process sequence embedded in quality systems in their implementation—**plan, do, check, act**—a process that is embedded in the corporate accountability management system called SA8000 (Social Accountability 8000), which focuses primarily on implementation of labour standards (Strum *et al.* 2000), but can be extended to TRM. The plan–do–check–act sequence provides a *process* for continual improvement which is needed to ensure not only that responsibility management is in place, but also that the company is on a path of continual improvement. Some of the considerations in the plan–do–check–act sequence, as applied to TRM, are noted below:

- **Plan.** Determine who are the relevant stakeholders and what are the related issues. Determine what standards are appropriate (i.e. for labour issues, check out ILO [International Labour Organisation] conventions and standards; for environmental issues, check out ISO 14000 and related standards; generally, focus on unique considerations for the particular stakeholder). Determine what the related laws, current global standards and principles, internal stakeholder expectations, and external stakeholder inputs and expectations (from the stakeholder engagement processes) are. Create a guiding coalition of representative internal stakeholders and management to oversee the process, develop responsibility goals and objectives related to stakeholders and environmental impacts, and obtain inputs from relevant stakeholders

- **Do**. Assess priorities based on current standards and internal documents. Determine where gaps exist between rhetoric and reality: that is, between the company's vision, mission and values statements and the way that stakeholders and the natural environment are treated through operating practices. Develop the specific measures relevant to each stakeholder and the natural environment; establish goals and objectives related to the responsibility vision, goals and values. Undertake a baseline study to determine the current status, including costs and benefits of changing practices, so that future results can be compared. Design and implement improvement programmes as necessary, including assignment of responsibility for implementation and results to specific parties, determination of operational and system controls. Provide employee (and other relevant) training as needed, assign responsibility where appropriate, and ensure that records are kept so that improvements and problems can be tracked

- **Check**. Have the guiding coalition review the results on a periodic basis, gathering relevant data and comparing it with baseline (or previous) results, as available. Communicate the results to relevant internal and external stakeholders for their feedback and ongoing assessment and engagement. Determine where problems still exist, where additional costs have been incurred and where improvements are still needed. Assess where improvements have been achieved and calculate benefits to relevant stakeholders

● **Act**. Revise responsibility goals, objectives and values as necessary. Revise programmes and practices as needed and where problems arise, to provide for a basis of continual improvement on responsibility measures. Issue a triple- or multiple-bottomline report to relevant stakeholders in the interests of transparency and accountability. Begin the cycle all over again, recognising that systemic change is ongoing and that no organisation is ever perfect, that improvements can always be made

Responsibility management, like quality management, means setting clear objectives to be achieved and articulating the values that drive the company's vision and strategies. We term this part of TRM *inspiration*, emphasising the vision and values-setting processes aimed at engaging stakeholders in the purpose of the organisation. Inspiration involves top managers making a public commitment to the company's vision and values, and it involves developing a vision for responsibility management that is widely shared so that leadership on issues of responsibility management can emerge at all levels of the organisation. Leaders, whatever their formal position, need to express willingness to engage with and learn from (and with) stakeholders whose interests in and commitments to the organisation create mutual investments and risks that are inevitably shared. In this respect, TRM is very similar to TQM, where topmanagement and leadership commitment to customers is a fundamental first step. The difference with TRM is that other stakeholders' interests also need to be taken into consideration.

There are other similarities between TRM and TQM. Quality management, it turned out, was not about an inspection at the end of the production line, as many people originally assumed. Rather, managing for quality ultimately meant changing all of the company's approaches and systems, *integrating* quality into the company's objectives, product/service and work standards, and changing the systems that support production and delivery to reflect the quality objectives. Much the same can be said of responsibility management. Once a company begins using the TRM framework, no system goes unchanged: the effects of managing responsibility ripple throughout the system. This ripple effect occurs because responsibility management is based on a holistic awareness of the enterprise as a living system. When you change one part of it, those changes ripple throughout the organisation.

Responsibility management, as with quality management, is not necessarily about perfection, but rather about a process of continual *improvement* and *innovation*. As with quality management, improving the company's responsibility management means *involving* and engaging with key stakeholders, particularly with employees. After all, it is employees who are charged with implementing the company's strategies and practices, and other stakeholders and the natural environment are affected by a company's strategies and practices. By engaging with them interactively, companies can develop *improvement* and *learning systems* that help them generate better returns and greater competitive advantage.

An old accounting saw goes, 'you get what you measure'. Yet quality can't be measured, or at least that was the initial response of many managers to the quality movement, who ultimately found numerous ways to measure quality. Today, we see similar responses around the issue of responsibility management. 'How do you measure improvements in responsibility management?' many managers ask. Or, 'you can't measure these things', they state. Despite the doubts, quality management systems, such as those promulgated by W. Edwards Deming, Joseph Juran and Philip Crosby, demonstrated clearly that measures of quality could indeed be developed. Similar advances in responsibility management measurement systems, what we term indicators, are now evolving.

In the most progressive companies today, managing quality is everyone's responsibility, not just the responsibility of a quality expert somewhere at the end of the line. A similar point can be made about managing responsibility. Unless responsibility management is *everyone's concern* and is devolved throughout the organisation, problems can arise unnoticed until it is too late and they are already in the public eye. This approach to managing responsibility goes well beyond public relations (or, as some people call it, window dressing), well beyond compliance and even well beyond the company's own boundaries into the supply and distribution chains. Taking responsibility for responsibility requires a systems orientation that touches all aspects of corporate life.

Managing responsibility is critical because, as NGOs, reporters and other corporate critics are likely to point out, it cannot be avoided. Some degree of responsibility—or irresponsibility—is present in every action or impact that a company has. Whether it is on the quality of work-life experienced by employees (whether in the home organisation or supply chain), the impacts that products and services have on customers, communities and even national cultures, or in the production systems' impacts on the natural environment, company activities have impacts. Increasingly, companies are being held accountable for the nature and quality of those impacts.

As with other management systems, such as quality, environmental and information management, responsibility management has to be thought through systemically and holistically. It is a *process* of building good stakeholder relationships through a continual improvement process that focuses on corporate practices, management systems, communication, strategies and transparency, much like quality management does. Responsibility management in one interpretation means engaging *interactively* with stakeholders in an open and transparent way, creating *explicit* responsibility management systems, and openly reporting results to interested parties. It recognises that there are no easy answers to dealing with the problems, criticisms and accusations directed at companies by various stakeholders, but that there *are* ways of managing that can help companies avoid problems in the first place, cope with them more effectively when they do arise and, ultimately, be more effective in their business operations.

Two things are critical in this regard. Responsibility management requires:

- **Building trusting and positive relationships with internal and external stakeholders** in order to be able to work productively through issues as they arise, rather than finding themselves the target of activism or negative journalism

- **Developing explicit and systemic management approaches for working through stakeholder and environmental issues**

2
The business case for responsibility management
THE NEW BUSINESS IMPERATIVE*

This section of the manual briefly discusses the rationale—or the business case—for managing corporate responsibility today. It reviews the key external pressures that have created the substantial stakeholder and environmental demands that companies now face and provides some evidence that building better relationships with stakeholders through the strategies and operating practices developed in TRM make good business sense.

* For an elaboration of the ideas in this section, see Waddock 2002 and Waddock *et al.* 2002.

2.1 Investor pressures

Companies necessarily pay attention to pressures from owners or investors, especially in nations where the shareholder is traditionally seen as the dominant stakeholder. During the 1980s and 1990s, a growing population of social investors began to exert significant pressures on companies to behave more responsibly with respect to certain issues, such as human rights, environmental performance and governance. Evidence of the concern about corporate responsibility by investors is highlighted in the fact that the Social Investment Forum has estimated that in the US alone more than US$2.29 trillion or one out of every eight equity dollars was invested in socially screened funds or equities.[1]

The Domini Index, for example, has tracked the performance of some 400 socially screened US companies since the early 1990s and typically outperformed traditional unscreened indices. The more recently developed Dow Jones Sustainability Index focuses on five principles related to corporate sustainability: innovative technology, corporate governance, shareholder relations, industrial leadership and social well-being, with the latter category explicitly emphasising positive corporate responsibility with respect to society. Following a similar path, the United Kingdom launched the FTSE4Good index in 2001. This new index emphasises environmental sustainability, positive stakeholder relationships, and upholding and supporting universal human rights. New laws in the UK and France, as well as increased attention in the European Union, focus attention on pension and mutual funds' transparency with respect to the social and ecological considerations embedded in their money management practices.

Further, the market slump and corporate scandals of the early 2000s revealed an interesting feature of social investment: many socially screened investment portfolios experienced investment inflows considerably above those of more traditional (unscreened) funds during the tough times of the early 21st century. The emergence of these indices, the

1 See the Social Investment Forum website for updates. This information is from the 2005 report, at www.socialinvest.org/areas/research/trends/sri_trends_report_2005.pdf (accessed December 2006).

shift to socially screened investments and the pressures arising from shareholder activists suggest growing investor interest in social screening on a global basis.

2.2 External assessments

The rise of interest in social investing has brought with it a corresponding capacity among social research firms, investment houses and large institutional investors to measure and evaluate corporate responsibility. Some 11 independent social research firms now belong to the Sustainable Investment Research International Company,[2] which combines the resources of the world's largest social investment research organisations. The SiRi Company has access to the results of more than 100 social research analysts, and taps their local knowledge of companies around the world.

Assessments of corporate responsibility undertaken by these social researchers follow quality guidelines developed by SiRi Company, and focus on multiple dimensions relevant to responsibility management. Some research emphasises specific issues, such as women's advancement, minority advancement, the environment, military contracting, involvement in so-called 'sin industries' and similar issues. Other social research on companies addresses stakeholder performance: for example, for employees, community relations, product quality (customers), and sustainability or environmental performance. Partly as a result of all of these evaluations, information about stakeholder relationships and how well companies are actually managing their responsibilities is now available to investors and, in some cases, published more widely in ratings and rankings (which will be discussed below). This information obviously goes well beyond the financial information traditionally available to investors and other stakeholders and is generally used by social investors interested in investing in companies whose values support their own values.

2 SiRi, www.siricompany.com.

Information on companies' stakeholder, social and environmental practices is increasingly becoming global through the efforts of research organisations such as SiRi Company. Consisting of the world's most noted social investment research firms, the international membership includes the leading firms in 11 different nations around the world, including Spain, Italy, Switzerland, the Netherlands, Sweden, Israel, the United States, Canada, the United Kingdom, Germany and Australia.[3] Over time this group hopes to cover all of the world's largest financial markets, harmonise their research products and systems, and develop national and transnational socially screened indices of companies. All of this will make information about company practices increasingly available—and transparent to a wide array of external stakeholders, including critics as well as investors, who are sometimes the same. Companies that recognise early on the shifting winds of transparent social, ecological and financial information can develop good stakeholder relationships through responsibility management and have a potential opportunity to gain the interest of the growing number of socially conscious investors.

2.3 Governance activism

Some corporate critics actually *become* investors for the explicit purpose of influencing corporate policy through the activism of shareholder resolutions. Shareholder resolutions, which are submitted to boards of directors for possible vote by investors in a firm, can address any number of different possible areas. Beginning in the late 1990s and continuing today, nearly 300 resolutions related to various aspects of corporate social policy are submitted annually by various groups and individuals interested in changing corporate policy. One such group in the US is the Interfaith Center on Corporate Responsibility (ICCR), which is an association of some 275 religious organisations. ICCR annually sponsors over 100 shareholder resolutions pushing companies to be more socially and environmentally responsible. Social policy shareholder activism in par-

3 www.siricompany.com/partners.shtml (accessed January 2007)

ticular has in recent years involved the submission of shareholder resolutions to management on issues of social concern by individual investors, large pension funds, social investors, labour unions and institutional investors, among others. Many companies work with shareholder activists directly to avoid becoming targets of shareholder resolutions or to take them 'off the table' prior to a shareholder vote.

2.4 Ratings and rankings

Another source of external pressure for managing responsibility is the numerous ratings and rankings of various corporate activities that now appear regularly. Ratings and rankings of corporate performance have grown in popularity in recent years. Such rankings offer lists of companies deemed the 'best' for different types of practice or for specific stakeholders, such as working women, minorities, most admired or best corporate citizens. Many of these rankings appear annually, some in very visible places, such as *Fortune* magazine, the *Financial Times*, *Business Ethics* magazine,[4] and similar publications. Best corporate citizens, most admired companies, reputational rankings based on stakeholder perceptions, best companies to work for, best companies for minorities, and so on create significant pressures for companies concerned about their reputation with important stakeholders, such as customers, investors and communities where they wish to locate facilities. One source of information about ratings and rankings and their impact on corporate reputation is The Reputation Institute at www.reputationinstitute.com.

Many companies pay close attention to their standing in these kinds of ranking, because they are based on customer perceptions, employee ratings and social research indicators, as well as the opinions of executives and financial analysts, all of which matter to important stakeholder groups. The visibility created by being high—or low—in a ranking creates a new degree of transparency around companies' stakeholder and environmental practices. This transparency in turn generates accounta-

4 Now *CRO* magazine.

bility by the company to specific stakeholders for the companies' impacts and practices. Stakeholder interest in these rankings represents a clear and emerging source of pressure emphasising the need for responsibility management.

2.5 Internet-fuelled activism

The large size, ability to garner resources, and power, impact and visibility of many of today's companies generates significant criticism and concern from non-governmental organisations, activists and trade unions. Over the past two decades, many companies have experienced a good deal of activism related to specific company policies, particularly with respect to globalisation, supply and distribution chain activities, and internal labour, human rights and environmental practices. Some companies have discovered to their distress that labour and human rights activists, environmentalists, and non-governmental organisations (NGOs) pay a *lot* of attention to supply chain practices that become increasingly visible through electronic communications technology. Much of today's transparency related to corporate practices and impacts exists because it takes only one or a few critical observers to spread negative news about a company—and the media is often all too eager to pick up on negative reports.

All of this visibility, of course, is facilitated by the internet, which provides a fast, efficient and effective means of disseminating information (or disinformation) about corporations and their practices, as well as mobilising activist interest in particular issues or problems. Websites devoted to poor corporate citizenship, such as sweatshops, human rights abuses or environmental problems created by companies, have become commonplace. In some instances, it only takes a single email in some listservs to generate significant interest in a corporate misdeed uncovered by an activist or NGO. This type of activism has reached the point where some companies are now buying up URLs with every conceivable negative name related to the company so that activist groups will not have access to those URLs. But even such aggressive policies are unlikely to stop activists who find no other meaningful routes to pressure companies for reforms.

2.6 Trade union activism

Labour and trade unions are increasingly aware of their power to raise important issues with respect to working conditions, especially those in developing nations. Members of trade unions are active in anti-globalisation and some anti-corporate protests around the world, fighting for economic justice for workers, better-paying jobs, a living wage in developing (and sometimes developed) nations and better working conditions, among other things. For example, one organisation called Labour Behind the Label in the UK has worked actively to draw attention to the situation of workers in garment factories around the world. In addition, this group emphasises retailers' responsibility for working conditions in the factories from which they source clothing and other goods.[5]

2.7 Consumer activism

Labour, human rights and environmental activists, fuelled by the connectivity of the internet, increasingly question the integrity of companies, particularly with respect to their outsourcing (notably labour and human rights) practices and ecological impacts, raising public awareness about such issues. The publicity attendant to demonstrations against global trade has resulted in more sophisticated consumers who increasingly demand that companies meet high expectations with respect to how and

5   For a list of activist organisations that includes the activities of some labour and trade groups, see the Directory of Groups and Organisations, Anti-Capitalism: A Guide to the Movement, www.tidsskriftcentret.dk/index.php?id=145 (accessed December 2006).

where their products are produced. These sophisticated consumers indicate in survey after survey that they make purchasing decisions based on (their perception of) a company's responsibility and citizenship (Rochlin and Christoffer 2000).

Although customers' actual purchasing behaviour may not yet fully reflect this growing awareness of corporate responsibility, many companies are aware of the need for proactive engagement with customers on important issues. Such engagement can be a means of developing relationships with customers (or what marketers call relationship marketing) and other stakeholders, such as employees, suppliers and communities, as a means of avoiding future problems. Of course, these consumer and other stakeholder relationships need to be based on trust—and it is in establishing that trust where responsibility management systems come into play, as we will discuss in later sections.

2.8 Standards and principles

Calls for corporate transparency and the corresponding accountability for corporate impacts are only likely to increase as activists, NGOs, environmentalists and investors become increasingly sophisticated about the extent to which companies actually live up to their stated values and visions. Similarly, such demands will increase as the internet provides ever more means of connecting interested stakeholders to the company. To build trust with stakeholders, it is important that corporate values align with internationally defined codes and standards, of which there has been an explosion in recent years.

Some of the most notable standards and principles generally agreed by the global community include the United Nations Declaration on Human Rights and the Environment, the International Labour Standards, the CERES principles, the Global Sullivan Principles, and the UN Global Compact. The latter's ten principles focus on human rights, labour rights and the environment, and signatories express voluntary agreement to live up to those principles.

Increasingly, businesses are expected by their stakeholders to articulate their own constructive visions guided by values, consistent with these emerging global principles and standards. In addition, activists expect companies to demonstrate that they are in reality *living up* to their espoused standards, which is where responsibility management processes can help.

2.9 Performance and managing responsibly

There is emerging evidence from academic and investor research that a strong business case can be made that responsible management practices and strong financial performance go hand in hand. Despite a general downturn in the financial markets in 2001, the Social Investment Forum found that socially and environmentally responsible mutual funds continued to outperform traditional, unscreened funds.[6] These results, as well as a significant body of empirical research by academics, call into question the traditional belief of the financial community that there is a necessary trade-off between responsible corporate performance and financial performance.

Evidence from scholars is mounting that the more responsible a company is in its strategies and operating practices, the better it is managed—and the better it performs financially. Considerable research now suggests that there is a positive link between corporate responsibility and the general quality of management, which leads to better financial performance.[7] Indeed, one study, called a meta-study because it reviews and combines the results of other studies, by Orlitzky and his colleagues, assessed

6 See www.socialinvest.org/areas/news/2001-Q2performance.htm (accessed December 2006).

7 For example, see Waddock and Graves 1997a, 1997b. For a recent review of the literature on the social–financial performance link, which concludes that the question is pretty much settled, see Margolis and Walsh 2003. A comprehensive quantitative meta-study with similar results was undertaken by Orlitzky *et al.* 2003.

the relationships found in 57 studies. These scholars found very strong positive relationships between responsibility and financial performance.

The linkages between more responsible practices and better financial performance and productivity come from a variety of sources and in many ways can be related to simple good management. For example, good management means taking good care of important resources, especially human resources, caring for them in all senses of the word. When employees are treated well, they will perform more effectively and overall results are likely to be better. In the responsible and well-managed company, tools and equipment are well cared for—and thus perform better and more efficiently. When less energy is wasted, when materials are recycled and re-used, when waste is reduced, the overall company is more efficient and productive—and more profitable. Similarly, customers who are treated well will return for repeat business, rather than being dissatisfied and telling their friends not to purchase from that company.

Employees treated well will reward the company with commitment and productivity. There will be less absenteeism, reduced turnover and more effort to improve operations. When they understand the broader vision and purpose of the firm, they will be better able to do their jobs well—and all of this is related not just to good management, but also to operating responsibly—respecting the employees as hard-working human beings willing and able to work for the good of the whole.

Further, some hidden or typically unrecognised costs can actually be reduced when responsible practices are implemented. For example, productivity may improve with better working conditions, environmental management can save resources and reduce waste, and management time can be spent on strategic issues rather than firefighting against activists who have raised concerns. And these are just a few ways in which responsibility management can be cost-effective.

3
Building integrity and sustainability systemically

Although every company's responsibility management system will differ, the TRM framework outlines the basic elements needed in any system. Each company's responsibility management system will be based on its particular stakeholders, market, industry and the cultural considerations specific to that company. Responsibility management is fundamentally about developing a company's *awareness* of its stakeholders, focusing on its responsibilities to those stakeholders and the natural environment, and implementing company-specific systems for managing those responsibilities while also yielding profits for the firm.

3.1 A process your company can use . . .

TRM allows companies to define their own responsibility management systems, developing a sense of the whole, articulating values to be put into practice through operating decisions and practices, and generating integrity goals that allow for long-term sustainability. What TRM mostly offers, then, is a *process*—a way of thinking about and ultimately managing *your* company's responsibilities.

TRM is also about the company's integrity, in the sense of forthrightness or honesty, soundness and wholeness. A key definition of integrity in this respect is 'adherence to a code': that is, a set of standards of practice, standards for responsibility that suggest a company knows what it stands for, what its values are—and how it wishes to make those values real through its practices. Openly engaging with responsibility management processes helps companies articulate what they stand for by focusing attention on the values that underpin action.

Responsibility management can be designed to meet a company's specific needs, industry and competitive situation, and strategic goals. And this approach provides a means by which managers can assess progress, innovation and improvement in meeting the company's overall goals and responsibilities, much as quality management systems provide information and feedback on how well a company meets customers' demands.

3.2 Improvement and innovation, but not perfection . . .

Responsibility management is not about perfection, but it is about improvement. TRM is about managing the company's relationships with different stakeholders, even critics. TRM is about processes of engagement, involvement and interaction. TRM is about establishing standards, goals and objectives so that the company can maintain its licence to operate today and its integrity in the eyes of employees, customers, communities and others tomorrow.

3.3 Integrity is the core . . .

The key to managing responsibility is building trust with important stake-holders. Trust can be built only when companies are forthcoming with information, even about problems. To be sustainable long-term, compa-nies need the trust of their stakeholders. To accomplish long-term sus-tainability demands integrity.

To build trust and operate with integrity, companies need to:

- Focus on *building relationships* with stakeholders
- Be worthy of the *trust* of their stakeholders over long periods of time
- *Work together with* their stakeholders rather than unilaterally
- Deal openly and honestly with stakeholders even when there are problems
- Be flexible and adaptive, taking multiple concerns and issues into account
- Be willing to listen to the concerns of others

3.4 Putting responsibility management into practice

There are many ways of managing a company's corporate citizenship or responsibility to help it to avoid problems. Some of these approaches can even create new opportunities for competitive advantage. Of course, the foundation is to have a sound vision that aims at a broader goal than sim-ply maximising shareholder wealth and actually emphasises how the company will play its part in building healthy societies or producing a bet-ter world. This vision is necessarily built on a sound ethical base, a base of articulated values which, as will be discussed below, help guide decision-making in the company—and avoid the sorts of problems besetting so many companies during the wave of frauds, accounting mis- or re-statements and problematic practices.

By *engaging with* stakeholders, rather than being in an adversarial relationship with them, by setting and keeping to standards of practice that have been globally agreed, and by working to continually improve corporate practices, companies can begin to achieve better stakeholder relationships, and potentially also better bottom-line results. They can generate new ideas and improve on old ones. They can improve productivity and performance, by engaging with the stakeholders who are responsible for implementation—the employees. They can build trustful, rather than adversarial, relationships with both internal and external stakeholders who might otherwise be critical of the company's actions and even thwart strategic initiatives.

In short, TRM like TQM provides standards and goals for strategy and implementation that are acceptable globally. In many cases, responsibility management can also improve productivity and bottom-line performance. These improvements come because any company's performance affects not just owners, but also other important stakeholders who are also making significant investments in the company.

Improving customer performance brings customers back for repeat business. Improving employee performance means higher retention, reduced training and recruitment costs, less absenteeism and, ultimately, better productivity. Better supplier and distributor relationships mean that systems for productivity, efficiency and supply chain management in general are enhanced. Better community relations mean fewer image and public relations nightmares, easier facility siting and improvement processes, and better working relationships with local governmental officials and neighbours. And all of this benefits the investor or owner in the form of better financial results.

Many of the costs associated with poor stakeholder and environmental performance and practices are hidden in traditional accounting systems. Yet there are costs, even if they have typically gone unmeasured. Responsibility management helps companies better determine what those costs are—and make changes and improvements that can reduce the costs and simultaneously improve performance.

As noted earlier, responsibility management approaches typically have four major processes associated with them: **inspiration** or vision-setting processes, **integration** of the responsibility vision and values into strategy and operating practices in all functions throughout the firm, plus **indicators** that measure and report on progress, so that **improvements** can be made. In the chapters that follow each of these components of responsibility management will be discussed in more depth, recognising that they are all part of the holistic approach to managing responsibility.

4

Inspiration

VISION SETTING AND COMMITMENT PROCESSES

Inspiration is all about establishing and ensuring that management makes a commitment to a company's vision and the values that underpin that vision. That is, inspiration is about the vision setting and management commitment processes. Inspiration involves developing a vision of how the company will interact with its stakeholders into the company's strategic vision and competitive strategies to make a difference in the world. The vision delineates the company's long-term goals and objectives, its strategies and the operating practices that will accomplish those strategies.

Inspiration is also a process that ensures top-management commitment to the responsibility management system. Inspiration determines the ways in which the company will engage with its stakeholders, sharing the vision, even developing it together. Inspiration, the vision setting and commitment process involves three major types of activity:

1. Creating and making a **company-wide commitment of top managers** and leaders throughout the enterprise to a corporate

vision, which includes its responsibilities with and to stakeholders

2. Articulating the company's **core values** and the ways in which those values link to the bedrock of internationally agreed **foundation values** that provide a *floor* of acceptable practice

3. **Engaging with key stakeholders** interactively to provide feedback and inputs necessary to shape the company's long-term vision and strategies

How companies that are implementing TRM think about them will be discussed in detail in the next chapters.

4.1 Inspirational vision: how do we change the world?

Company vision provides direction and guidance, making it clear what the company sees as its contribution to the world around it. It is in this sense of making a contribution to the world, not just producing profits for shareholders, that is found the inspiration that comes with vision, when it used for productive and positive purposes.

Inspirational visions create meaning for the company's employees and other stakeholders, particularly for employees who carry out the vision through their daily efforts. Because such visions incorporate the company's core values and articulate the types of relationship that companies hope to develop with their stakeholders, they also serve as a means of entering into an 'engagement' with those stakeholders.

Vision fosters a sense of purpose, both individual and community, when it is widely shared throughout the organisation.

4.2 Why does vision matter?

Vision matters because it guides the organisation and provides a way for people involved with the company to know what is important to it. Properly articulated and widely shared, vision can create a sense of community, of belonging. It can arguably also guide the organisation in the right direction, producing better results than would otherwise be achieved.

People have a fundamental need to belong and to make a contribution. In today's world, for many people being part of a company is an important way in which an individual's own purposes are fulfilled. Companies that are clear about what their fundamental vision is—that is, about how they will change the world—stand a better chance than less articulate companies of attracting productive and talented employees, retaining customers and working collaboratively with other important stakeholders. Inspirational vision helps people associated with a company understand their connection to the company—to belong, that is—and indicates how they can make a contribution. It also helps people figure out how their efforts on behalf of the company contribute to the world around them.

Vision helps a company articulate the fundamental strategic question: What are we in business to do? Answering this strategic question can provide guidance on how a company views its primary objectives and what it hopes to accomplish. To be effective, a vision needs to provide a sense of what the company hopes to accomplish in the future. Vision provides a sense of how the world will be different and, some would argue, better, because the company has done its work well. It is in the sense of illustrating an organisation's accomplishments and the meaning of its work that vision can be inspirational.

Thus, the most important thing that vision needs to do is provide a source of inspiration for key stakeholders such as employees. Vision needs to inspire, to create a sense of common purpose, so that people can feel that they are working toward a worthwhile end.

Vision means . . .

- To see with the eye what is and what might be present
- To imagine possibilities and potentials based on what currently exists

- To provide a positive 'picture' of the future

Vision can . . .

- Be a positive guide to action and for decision-making

- Help determine what should and should not be done

- Inspire people to do their best work

- Provide a meaningful framework for a company's stakeholders

- Create a sense of 'we' that inspires new ideas and contributions

- Provide a long-term sense of direction and purpose

The important work of James Collins and Jerry Porras (1997) highlights how a well-articulated vision can contribute to a company's long-term success. These researchers found that companies they called visionary outperformed non-visionary companies by more than 15 times over the long term.

Vision alone, however, is insufficient to guide action. Vision needs to be underpinned by values—core values that speak to the individuality of the company—as well as adherence to a core of internally agreed foundational values the provide the floor for any company's responsibility management system.

Indeed, in their book *Built to Last*, Collins and Porras found that the visionary companies that did so well had future-oriented, inspirational visions, supported by widely recognised core values along with supporting strategies that enabled the company to achieve its vision in the long term. It is to those values, both core to the company, and foundational to basic human dignity, that we now turn.

4.3 Defining values: what do we stand for?

A company's values shape its responsibility management and its commitments to stakeholders and the natural environment. Values determine management philosophy, which in turn shapes operating practices. It is in operating practices—the policies, procedures and processes that develop and deliver a company's goods and services and guide decision-making—that values are expressed in day-to-day terms. For better or worse, operating practices impact a company's stakeholders and the natural environment. Awareness of these impacts makes managers sensitive to the reactions and responses that different groups have to company decisions and actions.

Values are the principles, standards, ethics and ideals that companies (and people) live by. They shape the company's integrity and attention to stakeholders, as well the way in which the company's impacts, productivity and outputs are experienced by stakeholders, internally and externally.

Defining core values is an important part of managing responsibility because values dictate *how* a company interacts with its stakeholders, how it copes with its impacts and how it deals with problems. That question helps the company articulate its values and it is values that provide the ground on which practice is built. Some people call this second question the 'enterprise strategy question'. This question is: 'What do we stand for?'[1]

4.4 Company core values and foundation values

Companies implementing responsibility management approaches need to weigh two sets of core values: the company's own core values and a set of core foundation values that are based on internationally agreed standards that provide a floor below which it does not make sense to go. Though these values obviously may overlap to some extent, both types of value are important for different reasons.

---

1 This term is developed in Freeman and Gilbert 1988 and elaborated in Freeman *et al.* 2007.

4.4.1 Company core values

Core values are the basis of the company's capacity to operate with integrity. The company's core values are important because they help define what is important and specific to the particular company. As noted above, they help answer the question: What do we stand for?

In their work on visionary companies, for example, Collins and Porras (1997) pointed out that the visionary company's 'core ideology' comprised both the company's vision and its core values.

Some examples of core values in some of the companies Collins and Porras studied are (Collins and Porras 1997: 68-71):

- 3M: Innovation—'Thou shall not kill a new product idea'; absolute integrity; respect for individual initiative and personal growth; tolerance for honest mistakes; product quality and reliability; 'Our real business is solving problems'

- American Express: heroic customer service; worldwide reliability of service; and encouragement of individual initiative

- Merck: 'We are in the business of preserving and improving human life. All of our actions must be measured by our success in achieving this goal'; honesty and integrity; corporate social responsibility; science-based innovation, not imitation; unequivocal excellence in *all* aspects of the company; profit, but profit from work that benefits humanity

- Procter & Gamble: Product excellence; continuous self-improvement; honesty and fairness; respect and concern for the individual

Determining what values are really 'core' to a company is an important process that needs to involve many internal stakeholders (particularly employees at all levels). It is important to note a couple of things that are really important as you explore your own company's core values:

- Core values need to be truly that: core. Core means those values are the ones that your company will sustain over a long period of time no matter what happens

- There are only a *few* values that can be core

The 'what do we stand for?' question can only be answered effectively through an exploration of the company's history, traditions and important strategies, from which can be derived those values considered to be 'core' to that company. Questions that can be asked of employees, managers and top management, as well as external stakeholders who know the company well (i.e. suppliers, customers and local communities), include:

- What do you see as the core principles by which this company operates?

- What values are really important here?

- What do you think the founding principles of this company are?

- What standards and operating principles would we *never* give up?

The values that consistently appear on lists or in conversations of groups of individuals associated with the firm are probably the firm's core values. Such values are relatively immutable: that is, they are consistent over long periods of time. They are fairly constant. And they really represent what the company does, in fact, stand for in ways that individuals familiar with the company will readily recognise.

4.4.2 Foundation values

Foundation values are generally agreed standards and principles that provide a floor of acceptable practice, going below which makes little sense and can create significant managerial and reputational problems for companies. Generally speaking, foundation values emphasise certain major areas:

- Respect for human dignity in and out of the workplace

- Respect for basic rights, including labour and human rights

- Respect for the long-term viability of human civilisation in the natural environment

- Respect for the role of the company *as part of* the broader societies in which it operates

- Respect for the integrity of the company and the systems within which it operates

Many of these foundation principles find their expression in the three-pronged focus of the United Nations Global Compact initiative, which asks companies to sign on and live up to a set of ten principles related to human rights, labour standards, the environment and anti-corruption. These principles follow along the lines of the triple bottom line of social (human rights principles), economic (labour rights principles) and ecological principles that will be discussed in Chapter 7.

The Global Compact's ten principles are listed in Box 4.1.

The Global Compact's ten principles are based on internationally agreed standards found in documents such as the UN Declaration on Human Rights and the Environment, the International Labour Organisation's Declaration on Fundamental Principles and Rights at Work, the UN's Agenda 21 (the Rio Declaration on Environment and Development), the UN Convention Against Corruption, and related documents. As documents that have been agreed to by the majority of the world's nations, they represent a broad-based consensus on the minimal standards needed for businesses operating in the global arena.

The original Global Compact consisted of nine principles. The tenth principle against corruption was added in 2004 in recognition of the important work needed to reduce corruption in governments and businesses. Transparency International suggested the need for what that organisation calls **system integrity**. System integrity arises out of the capacity for trust in the soundness and honesty of the governmental and economic systems. Foundation principles associated with system integrity, according to Transparency International, are:

- Participation
- Decentralisation
- Diversity
- Accountability
- Transparency

PRINCIPLES OF THE GLOBAL COMPACT

Kofi Annan, Secretary-General of the United Nations, called in 1999 for companies to live up to the following principles:

HUMAN RIGHTS

Principle 1: support and respect the protection of international human rights within their sphere of influence

Principle 2: make sure their own corporations are not complicit in human rights abuses

LABOUR

Principle 3: freedom of association and the effective recognition of the right to collective bargaining

Principle 4: the elimination of all forms of forced and compulsory labour

Principle 5: the effective abolition of child labour

Principle 6: the elimination of discrimination in respect of employment and occupation

ENVIRONMENT

Principle 7: support a precautionary approach to environmental challenges

Principle 8: undertake initiatives to promote greater environmental responsibility

Principle 9: encourage the development and diffusion of environmentally friendly technologies

ANTI-CORRUPTION

Principle 10: Businesses should work against all forms of corruption, including extortion and bribery

Box 4.1

Source: The Global Compact, www.unglobalcompact.org/AboutTheGC/TheTenPrinciples/index.html

It is worth noting that there are similar values underlying many of the organisational initiatives, as well as the numerous codes of conduct both internal to companies and externally generated that have been undertaken in the past several decades to improve corporate performance. Some of the similarities in what are believed to be good management practices can be derived from common principles and approaches found in a variety of management approaches used to better the company, including quality management, strategic thinking, re-engineering, participative management, and related improvement initiatives that companies have undertaken. These principles, drawn from the work of management scholar Jeanne Liedtka, are listed in Table 4.1.

These practices and their associated values have been linked with improved organisational performance in the numerous initiatives from which they are derived. Like other approaches intended to improve performance, responsibility management approaches are:

- Holistic and systemic
- Cross-functional
- Integrative and integrity-oriented
- Empowering of employees in particular, as well as other stakeholders
- Process-oriented
- Values-based and -driven
- Oriented towards creating meaning and purpose
- Based on integrity
- Based on interactive engagement

The case of the Swiss Clean Clothes Campaign (see Box 4.2) explores the ways in which foundational values play an important role in developing a sustainable relationship between companies and a grass-roots campaign.

SHARED THEMES	RELEVANT VALUES-BASED PRACTICES
Create a shared sense of meaning, vision and purpose that connects the personal to the organisational	• Values community without subordinating the individual • Sees community purpose as flowing from individuals
Develop a systems perspective: a view held by each individual of him- or herself as embedded within a larger system	• Seeks to serve other community members and ecosystem partners
Emphasise business processes, rather than hierarchy or structure	• Believes work itself has intrinsic value • Belief in quality of both ends and means
Localise decision-making around work processes	• Responsibility for actions • Primacy of reach, with needed support
Leverage information within the system	• Truth telling (honesty, integrity) • Full access to accurate and complete information
Focus on development, at both personal and organisational levels	• Value the individual as an end • Focus on learning and growth, at both individual and organisational levels
Encourage dialogue	• Freedom and responsibility to speak and to listen • Commitment to find higher ground through exchange of diverse views
Foster the capacity to take multiple perspectives simultaneously	• Willingness to understand and work with the perspectives of others, rather than imposing own views
Create a sense of commitment and ownership	• Promise keeping • Sense of urgency • Engagement rather than detachment

TABLE 4.1 Values-based management practices in systems approaches to managing

Sources: adapted from Liedtka 1998 in Waddock 2006

FOUNDATIONAL VALUES

CORPORATE–CIVIL SOCIETY PARTNERSHIP: THE SWISS CLEAN CLOTHES CAMPAIGN AND CODE OF CONDUCT IMPLEMENTATION

Corporations are increasingly looking to NGOs for strategic partnerships and expertise in the area of corporate responsibility. One booming area for corporate and civil society co-operation is in code of conduct implementation. This case documents a structured collaboration in this area arising from a grass-roots campaign initiated by the Swiss Clean Clothes Campaign (CCC) and a group of European retailers.

INITIATIVE HISTORY AND BACKGROUND

In 1995 three Swiss NGOs (L'Action De Carême, Bern Declaration and Pain pour la Prochain, known as the Swiss Clean Clothes Campaign) began campaigning on working conditions in the sports industry. As part of these initiatives the Swiss CCC launched a consumer campaign in the late 1990s targeting 15 companies advocating for more transparency. The Swiss CCC's primary purpose was advancing the interests of workers in the apparel and sportswear industry. In 1999, from this initial grass-roots activism, three Swiss retailers separately approached the Swiss CCC to develop a longer-term relationship. The impetus for the retailers in this civil-society collaboration was to create a more proactive strategy regarding increasingly contentious issues, such as supply chain management and workers' rights.

COMPANY COMMITMENT TO CODES OF CONDUCT

The Swiss CCC believed that committing to changes in purchasing practices would be likely to produce the greatest improvements in workers' rights. In order to encourage this change in workers' rights, the Swiss CCC helped establish a new legal association with a board composed of members from each of the three NGOs and the three

Box 4.2 (continued opposite)

companies. This group then hired an expert consultant to help the firms introduce the appropriate systems needed for responsible supply chain management.

The board's second action step was authorising the code of conduct principles for the participating companies. The code provided a concise statement of minimum labour standards set forth in the four core ILO conventions regarding child labour, forced labour, freedom of association and freedom from discrimination. The participating companies pledged to observe these standards and to require its contractors, subcontractors, suppliers and licensees to observe them as well. Additionally, the companies who signed on to the code pledged to permit independent and external monitoring of the code. This commitment illustrates two fundamental concepts of TRM. The first is the incorporation of international standards and the second is commitment to measurement systems, which in the CCC project was accomplished by independent and external monitoring.

On 31 March 2000 the three Swiss retail companies accepted the standards of the Swiss CCC code for production of garments and shoes. These commitments became the platform for the pilot project between the Swiss CCC and the retailers beginning in the same year. By accepting the Swiss CCC standards the companies were adopting a company-wide vision for responsible supply chain practices, a fundamental aspect of TRM. Also, by entering into this agreement supporting workers' rights with the Swiss CCC, the companies demonstrated top-management commitment, another critical element of TRM.

The essential TRM process of stakeholder engagement between companies and the civil-society organisation Swiss CCC was brought to a new level in the summer of 2000. The retailers and the Swiss CCC initiated a $1\frac{1}{2}$ year project with four major aims. The first was to test the feasibility of external and independent monitoring of a code of conduct and focused primarily on business labour practices. Second, the project was designed to give support and assist in the creation of a network of partners in production countries who are willing and have the capacity to participate in independent monitoring. Third, the Swiss CCC sought to participate in developing educational materials on workers' rights or suppliers, partners and workers—in essence,

Box 4.2 (from previous page; continued over)

capacity building in the TRM framework. Finally, the pilot project sought to encourage collaboration with similar initiatives through Europe such as the Ethical Trading Initiative (ETI) in the UK, the Fair Wear Charter Foundation in the Netherlands, Ethique sur L'Etiquette in France and the Swedish Project on Independent Verification.

As part of the pilot project, the Swiss CCC drafted a work plan designed to explain and assign the roles for all participants (the companies, the board and the consultant), as well as timelines for specific action steps. This covered the entire project from the initial operation of the code of conduct through external evaluation of suppliers in test sites. By drafting this work plan, the parties developed clarity on strategies and goals, an important step in TRM that helps integrate responsibility ideals, such as workers' rights, into management systems. Then the board selected two testing locations in India and China where they would implement the pilot project with one supplier from each participating company.

MOVING THE CODE FROM COMPANIES TO SUPPLIERS

After endorsing the code of conduct at the company level, the next commitment of participating companies required their selected suppliers to endorse the code of conduct. For some companies this meant actually documenting all the suppliers. This involved recording details such as the name of the supplier, commercial status of the firm, nationality of supplier, importance of the firm to the supplier and vice versa. Once all suppliers had been identified they were sent copies of the code to sign. For compliance with the initiative, the companies needed to chart the responses and update the external consultant on a regular basis until the task had been completed. The Swiss CCC campaign used its newsletter as a carrot-and-stick incentive by publishing articles updating its readers on the companies' progress with this step. In addition, new suppliers wanting to source to the participating companies were asked to endorse the code of conduct as part of the terms of business; those who would not sign the agreement would not be considered appropriate partners.

Now companies are at the phase of developing and implementing training programmes for their own buyers, and their suppliers are

Box 4.2 (from previous page; continued opposite)

developing training to inform their workers on the details of the code. These types of training are intended to help build internal and supplier capacity, a central tenet of TRM, in this case to address workers' rights.

In 2003 the pilot project finished monitoring three supplier sites in India and China from the three participating companies. These reports as well as all major pilot project documents can be found at www.somo.nl/monitoring/initiatives/ch_eng_summ.htm (accessed December 2006).

LESSONS LEARNED IN CORPORATE–CIVIL SOCIETY COLLABORATION

Knowledge sharing through the consultant provided participating companies with relevant information from the other companies participating in the pilot project and their best practices without infringing on confidentiality. The consultant structure also provided more individualised coaching in challenging areas for companies without fear of reprisal from activists. Also, the reporting process to the consultant kept constant pressure on the companies to move forward with commitments while juggling all the other equally pressing responsibilities.

The limited scope of the initiative has proved to be both supportive in some areas and constraining in others. By setting very specific targets and action plans in the beginning, all participants had clear expectations. The process of identifying local partners, as well as developing training and supportive materials, has taken more time than initially expected. Also, a considerable amount of the consultant's effort was needed to track the reports required by companies as the terms of participation in the pilot project.

Box 4.2 (from previous page)

4.4.3 Pushing the TQM–TRM link

As can readily be seen in Table 4.2, many of the core values of managing for quality as expressed, for example, in the criteria for the United States Baldrige Quality Award are similar to core values in TRM. These core concepts and values provide specific action guides for managers interested in developing their own responsibility management systems.

4.5 Why do vision and values matter?

The uniqueness of every company's situation means that there is no single set of values or standards that, at least today, applies to all companies. Rather, responsibility management is built on a foundation of generally agreed values, such as the ILO conventions on labour and human rights *combined with* the basic individuality of company visions, strategies and commitments. Companies implementing responsibility management approaches develop company-specific approaches to responsible management that provide a framework to guide managers, without putting unnecessary constraints on their activities.

Vision setting and leadership systems create the organisational context for managing responsibility. A necessary condition is having a clear vision about corporate responsibility from top management and well-articulated guiding core values that support the vision. Further, as research on the implementation of codes of conduct in multinational supply chains indicates, top management needs to make a clear, consistent and repeated commitment to both the vision and the values or they will not 'take'.

Ensuring that a company's own vision embeds the company's core values and its responsibilities to (and with) its stakeholders, as well as foundation values, helps a company achieve its strategic objectives. Articulating these values is an important element in developing a coherent and meaningful vision and strategy. Meaningful strategies with constructive values *inspire* employees to work hard, *inspire* customers to purchase the company's products and services, and *inspire* communities to want the

BALDRIGE AWARD CORE VALUES/CONCEPTS	TRM CORE VALUES/CONCEPTS
Visionary leadership Sets direction, creates customer focus, clear and visible values, and high expectations	**Visionary and committed leadership** Sets direction of vision, clearly articulated and constructive values, and high expectations about responsible practices with respect to all stakeholders, but particularly employees, and for the consequences of corporate impacts on the natural environment
Customer-driven excellence Quality and performance are judged by customers	**Stakeholder-driven excellence and responsible practices** Responsibility and performance are judged by stakeholders, especially employees, customers, supplier/allies and owners
Organisational and personal learning Includes continuous improvement of existing approaches and adaptation to change, leading to new goals and approaches, embedded in daily operations organisationally and individually	**Organisational and personal learning through dialogue and mutual engagement with relevant stakeholders** Includes stakeholder engagement processes that provide a forum for continual learning and improvement of corporate practice
Valuing employees and partners Success depends on knowledge, skills, creativity and motivation of employees and partners	**Valuing employees, partners, other stakeholders** Success depends on knowledge, skills, creativity, motivation and engagement of employees, partners and relevant other stakeholders on issues related to corporate practices and impacts

TABLE 4.2 Comparison of core values and concepts in TQM/Baldrige Award and TRM (continued over)

Source: Baldrige National Quality Program 2001, Criteria for Performance Excellence, www.quality.nist.gov/2001_Criteria.pdf.htm, accessed September 2004

BALDRIGE AWARD CORE VALUES/CONCEPTS	TRM CORE VALUES/CONCEPTS
Agility Success demands a capacity for rapid change and flexibility	**Agility and responsiveness** Success demands a capacity for rapid change, flexibility and responsiveness when stakeholder-related issues or problems arise
Focus on the future (short and long term) Pursuit of sustainable growth and market leadership requires a strong future orientation and willingness to make long-term commitments to key stakeholders, customers, employees, suppliers and partners, stockholders, the public and your community	**Focus on the future (short and long term)** Pursuit of sustainable growth and market leadership requires a strong future orientation and willingness to respect and make long-term commitments to key stakeholders, customers, employees, suppliers and partners, stockholders, the public, your community and the natural environment
Managing for innovation Making meaningful change to improve products, services, and processes, and to create new value for stakeholders	**Managing for responsibility and improvement** Making meaningful change to ensure that practices that produce products and services are responsible, respectful and value-creating for key stakeholders
Management by fact Measurement and analysis of performance, derived from business needs and strategy, providing data about key processes, outputs and results	**Management by fact, transparency, accountability** Measurement, evaluation and transparency of the responsibility of corporate stakeholder and ecological practices, providing data about the responsibility that is integral to corporate practices, outputs and impacts

TABLE 4.2 (from previous page; continued opposite)

BALDRIGE AWARD CORE VALUES/CONCEPTS	TRM CORE VALUES/CONCEPTS
Public responsibility and citizenship Leaders should stress public and citizenship responsibilities, including meeting basic expectations related to ethics and protection of public health, safety and environment	**Public responsibility and citizenship** Leaders should assure that corporate practices related to economic, societal and ecological bottom lines are responsible, ethical and transparent to relevant stakeholders and hold themselves accountable for their positive and negative impacts
Focus on results and creating value Performance measures should focus on key results, and be used to create and balance value for key stakeholders—customers, employees, stockholders, suppliers and partners, the public and the community	**Focus on positive results, impacts and value-added for stakeholders with responsible ecological practices** Performance measures should focus on key results, and be used to create and balance value for key stakeholders—customers, employees, stockholders, suppliers and partners, the public, the community, and the natural environment

TABLE 4.2 (from previous page; continued over)

BALDRIGE AWARD CORE VALUES/CONCEPTS	TRM CORE VALUES/CONCEPTS
Systems perspective The core values and seven Baldrige criteria provide a systems perspective for managing an enterprise, forming the building blocks and integrating mechanism for the system, which, however, requires organisation-specific synthesis and alignment. • Synthesis means looking at your organisation as a whole and building on key business requirements, strategic objectives and action plans • Alignment means using key linkages among categories to provide key measures and indicators of success	**Systems perspective on responsible management practices** TRM's core values and criteria provide a framework for developing responsible management practices that can help a company integrate responsibility into all of its stakeholder and ecological practices, in alignment with the goals, objectives, values and strategy of the organisation. • Integration means that responsibility is inherent or integral in corporate practices and cannot be dissociated from them. Integration means that management recognises the responsibility that is inherent to practices and actions that affect stakeholders or nature and works to reduce negative impacts • Alignment means using key linkages and indicators to determine how stakeholders and nature are affected by corporate practices and actions

TABLE 4.2 (from previous page)

company to locate nearby, among other ways in which they can help a company become more effective.

Values thus provide a way for stakeholders to align themselves with the company and ensure that common interests and concerns are met. They are also, when constructive, a source of meaningful connection that provides a kind of social 'glue' among important constituents.

4.6 The importance of being real . . .

One caveat: values need to be real not just rhetoric. Trust, respect and integrity are important elements of developing ongoing relationships between companies and stakeholders. Company reputation is built on this trust, reputation and integrity, not just on public relations or image. Thus, companies need to think carefully about what their values *really* are because their stakeholders pay attention. When there is a gap between the stated and the actual values, employees, customers, community members and activists easily become sceptical.

For example, employees look to what top managers say—and, more importantly, what they do and what they reward—for guidance in their own behaviour. If employees, or critical outsiders such as activists or customers, believe that an apparent commitment to values is merely a public relations exercise, then there is little real hope that it will become integrated into a company's operating practices sufficiently to make a difference. And the key, as the next section will discuss, to making values real is gaining management commitment to the responsibility vision and values a company hopes to achieve.

The Statoil case in Box 4.3 illustrates the importance of inspiration through the vision setting process, including gaining top-management commitment, establishing core values and engaging interactively with the company's stakeholders, which will be discussed below.

INSPIRATION AND STAKEHOLDER ENGAGEMENT
STATOIL AND ICEM:
INCREASING GLOBAL WORKERS' RIGHTS

In 1998, Statoil became the first international company to sign a global agreement on human rights, industrial relations, and health and safety issues with an international trade union, International Federation of Chemical, Energy, Mine and General Workers' Union (ICEM), and a Norwegian workers' union (NOPEF). This innovative collaboration had both unexpected benefits and challenges that were addressed during the negotiation of the agreement. In creating this agreement Statoil took actions to develop a shared vision through stakeholder engagement demonstrating several components of TRM.

COMPANY HISTORY AND BACKGROUND

Statoil ASA is one of the world's largest net sellers of crude oil, and a substantial supplier of natural gas to Europe. It is also a leading Norwegian retailer of petrol and other oil products. Statoil independently, and in participation with other companies, carries out exploration, production, transport, refining and marketing of petroleum and petroleum-derived products, as well as other business. Statoil, with its 25,644 employees, operates in 33 countries throughout Europe, North America, South America and Asia (www.statoil.com, accessed December 2006).

MUTUAL ENGAGEMENT: FORGING NEW RELATIONSHIPS

Companies in the extraction industries, such as Statoil, face a number of challenges such as strong competition, environmental regulations and major safety concerns. In 1997 the 20 million-strong ICEM and NOPEF approached Statoil to broker the first ever global agreement on labour and human rights between an international company and international trade union. This type of agreement marked a departure from traditional contract-oriented industrial labour agreements solely between employers and employee associations. Since Statoil was increasing operations at the international level, its leaders thought it

Box 4.3 (continued opposite)

would be more efficient to have a direct relationship with an international union that had experience in nearly all the countries in which Statoil operated or wished to in the future.

In the spring of 1998 top union officials from ICEM, NOPEF and Statoil management held a number of meetings to discuss the parameters of the proposal. One of the initial sticking points was the unions' desire to specify limits on working hours in all country operations. In the initial meetings the parties realised that the global agreement should not interfere with locally negotiated agreements. Furthermore, it was determined that this accord should not be a traditional tariff agreement since contracts are typically best arranged through local agreements between employers and employee associations. With this essential clarification, the parties moved away from a collective bargaining contract towards a new form of union–business relationship, which focused on information exchanges, about how to work together and on how to improve working practices within operations. Although initiated by ICEM, this negotiation demonstrated Statoil's commitment to act as a collaborator with the unions. This process allowed the unions to define their terms of engagement with the company in this innovative contract, an essential element of the TRM stakeholder engagement.

INSPIRATION: THE STATOIL VISION

In the accord, both parties committed to uphold basic human rights in their communities and in their workplaces. Specifically, the agreement added basic worker rights by endorsing the International Labour Organisation (ILO)'s Fundamental Principles and Rights at Work. The ILO has established eight principles in four core areas (matched by those of the Global Compact) as fundamental labour standards. Core ILO standards encompass: (1) freedom of association; (2) the ability to engage in collective bargaining; (3) a commitment not to employ forced or bonded labour; and (4) a commitment to avoid child labour. The Statoil commitment and contract included management–employee training to support the initiative and monitoring by the unions. In fact, since 1998 ICEM has undertaken a performance assessment of Statoil through an annual survey of local unions in each

Box 4.3 (from previous page; continued over)

country in which the company operates. In addition to these pledges, the accord included an annual review meeting to assess the implementation of the agreement and the opportunity to discuss matters related to HSE, corporate policy, the fiscal position of the company, training, issues affecting the rights endorsed in the agreement and other mutually agreed topics. Both the union survey and annual meetings allow for feedback and assessment, critical elements involved in the innovation and learning about how well responsibility, in this case for employees, is being managed.

As envisioned, relationships between the unions and management have improved greatly, as is evident by the increasing flow of information between Statoil and its employees. Because of this agreement employees have the ability to speak directly to the company regarding issues involved in the accord and no longer have to go through intermediaries. Another example of the strengthened institutional-level relationships is that ICEM invited Statoil to speak at their world conference on oil about their joint agreement. This presentation was given in front of an audience of unions and other multinationals and allowed ICEM to demonstrate through role modelling to local managers that such agreements are possible and can improve relationships between employees and management since they provide an open channel for discussion.

INTEGRATION AND IMPLEMENTATION

Following the initial stages of collaboration, Statoil and ICEM began to focus on more practical ways to see that the agreement is implemented throughout Statoil's operations. One of the first steps in this implementation process was the training in human rights for union delegates in Azerbaijan. The goal of the training was to begin to share how Statoil implements human rights ideas in Norway and how it co-operates with the unions, essentially giving the Azerbaijanian colleagues a flavour of how good partnership can be designed and without being a strict formula for action. In autumn 2001, meetings between ICEM and Statoil managers were held on environment, health and safety (EHS) in order to go through their mandates, decide on priorities and how implement them. As a follow-up the company

Box 4.3 (from previous page; continued opposite)

published its first corporate social responsibility report in 2002 and maintains an in-house human rights awareness and training program for staff that is provided by Amnesty International. In 2003, Statoil became one of the founders of a new initiative called the Business Leaders Initiative on Human Rights, a three-year effort to help lead and develop corporations' responses to human rights issues.

LESSONS LEARNED

Direct company–union agreements can complement local agreements. Through discussion new types of agreement between international unions and multinational organisations can expand collaboration, while maintaining traditional collective bargaining.

Direct agreements can lead to better stakeholder relationships. This leads to more information sharing between these institutions and individual employees.

Box 4.3 (from previous page)

4.7 Leadership commitment

Leaders and managers in a company play a crucial role in developing vision and values. Adopting a TRM approach means systemically changing the entire company, ensuring that vision and values are integrated into all of a company's strategies and operating practices, and, as the Statoil case illustrates, also requires top-management involvement. As with quality management processes, successful responsibility management systems require the ongoing support and commitment of the leadership and management team if they are to be accepted and integrated throughout the company.

Consistent communication about the need for responsibility in a company's operations and all of its dealings with employees, suppliers, communities and customers (among others) is important—and that communication needs to come right from the top-management team and be infused throughout the company through the company's systems and policies. Many quality improvement initiatives have foundered on a lack of management support and much the same can be said of responsibility management. Unless there is clear and consistent guidance from the top—and from wherever leadership is exerted in the organisation—employees and others are unlikely to believe in the reality of the company's commitment to its responsibility vision or its values.

Here are some of the considerations that leaders of companies wishing to implement responsibility management need to consider so that they can overcome obstacles to the needed changes in a company's systems and practices. Leaders, wherever they are in the organisation, but particularly in top management, need to:

- **Take a long-term perspective.** Making a commitment to a responsibility vision and accompanying objectives requires a long- rather than a short-term orientation. In the short term it may seem as though committing to responsibility management requires trade-offs between immediate results and profitability. In the short term it can appear that lower-cost wages resulting from poor working conditions or poor environmental practices that result in pollution and the externalisation of environmental control practices can result in better profitability. From a longer-term perspective, however, the real costs of poorly trained and unskilled employees or environmental clean-up become more obvious. These costs are evident in the loss of customer satisfaction with quality, reduced employee productivity, and costs associated with pollution, safety concerns and compliance problems. Leaders with vision know that responsibility management needs to be considered in the medium to longer term rather than just the short term

- **Make a public commitment**. Leaders throughout the organisation need to publicly state their commitment to the responsibility vision and the practices that are needed to support it and make it real

- **Communicate the commitment.** Once the public commitment has been made by leaders, it needs to be communicated widely and frequently to all units within the company, including the companies in the supply chain that are intimately associated with the contracting firm. The key is to communicate, communicate, communicate the vision and values in every message that the company delivers, whether to investors, employees, customers, suppliers or others who work closely with the company

- **Be a role model for the company's values.** Rhetoric will not be enough. Once the vision, values and responsibility objectives are identified and communicated, leaders at all levels need to ensure that they exemplify in word and deed those values. Inconsistency about the vision and values sends all kinds of mixed messages

- **Integrate vision and values into strategies and practices.** The key to successful implementation of TRM rests in the extent to which the identified vision and values are actually integrated into the company's strategies, systems and the operating practices that affect stakeholders. This topic will be discussed extensively in the next chapter; however, it is clear that leadership commitment to this integration process can help close any gaps that might exist that send mixed messages between stated values and reality

Leaders need to pay particular attention to ensuring that the responsibility vision, values and goals are linked to:
- Strategy and strategic initiatives
- Reward systems
- Labour and human resource systems and standards
- Cross-functional teams and projects
- Product/service quality
- Customer relationships
- Corporate integrity
- Community relationships
- Environmental practices
- Reporting systems, which need to be both transparent and provide for accountability

● **Support change.** Leaders particularly need to acknowledge the difficulties of change—and find ways to help support staff through the changes that will inevitably be needed to move towards fulfilling the company's responsibility goals and achieving its vision

The importance of leadership commitment is clear from the vignette in Box 4.4.

4.8 Stakeholder engagement

Finding inspiration from vision and values allows a company to move forward. But what really helps in this process is determining what stakeholders, both internal and external, think of the company and its efforts. Getting feedback from engaging with stakeholders and using that feedback to help make improvements is a critical part of the continual improvement process associated with responsibility management.

There are several key steps to understanding stakeholder engagement and the role that it plays in managing responsibility:

LEADERSHIP AND COMMITMENT BY TOP MANAGEMENT

The CEO of a leading sports company gave a speech on the company's primary objectives. Despite nascent activities in responsibility management, the speech was noticeably lacking in any discussion about the company's responsibility objectives. This fact was duly—and publicly—noted by the company's many critics and highlights one of the key points of creating a responsibility management system: the need for top-management leadership and commitment in creating a values-driven vision for the company.

Box 4.4

1. Determine how to move the company to an interactive—or engaged—stance with respect to its stakeholders

2. Identify the important stakeholders and stakeholder groups

3. Set up processes to engage stakeholders. These processes include establishing appropriate two-way communication channels and systems that allow stakeholders to engage and be engaged in a mutual process of problem-solving and issue clarification and resolution

4. Communicate results to stakeholders and keep them engaged over time without 'exhausting' their goodwill

4.8.1 Move the company to an interactive engaged stance

Companies have choices about how to relate to their stakeholders. Three very different 'stances' or postures can be taken:

- Reactive
- Proactive
- Interactive

Reactive stance

Companies taking a reactive posture wait until a stakeholder—for example, an employee, customer, supplier, or member of a community or government—raises a particular issue or problem. Then they react based on their current strategy or ongoing initiatives.

This reactive posture can leave a company vulnerable, because the company may be unprepared to really deal with the issue in the moment. For example, many companies were caught unaware in the early 1990s when, as they attempted to globalise the sourcing of their products, they found activists criticising them strongly and publicly for poor labour practices in the companies with which they were contracting. Because they had little experience with managing supplier relationships to meet emerging global standards, they often reacted to the criticism in ways that brought on more problems than they started with. Similarly, many of the companies caught up in scandal seem to have passively allowed misdeeds to go on without taking the necessary forward-looking actions to forestall them.

Proactive stance

Companies that are proactive attempt to understand and address problems before they arise. Frequently, they do this by scanning the environment, thinking about what problems might be raised, and attempting to put policies or programmes in place that will avert those problems. They may put in place a code of conduct or significant programmes for ethics and values-training, and install reward systems that actually take performance with respect to stakeholders into account. For example, companies that anticipate problems in siting a facility may initiate a corporate philanthropy programme to build community relations in advance of actually entering a community. Or companies that have had problems with product quality in the past may establish a customer relations function to handle customer enquiries and complaints better. Such functions, sometimes called boundary-spanning functions, can begin the process of building relationships with key stakeholders because at least those stakeholders have someplace to go in the company with their concerns.

Stakeholder engagement: an interactive stance

As good as the proactive stance is in its attempt to anticipate and hence respond to problems before they arise, it is still largely premised on one-way communication: company *to* stakeholder. Many companies are finding that two-way communication or what is called stakeholder engagement can help provide better information about possible problems and better prepare the company for issues.

Stakeholder *engagement* is an interactive, dialogue-based and mutual process between companies and their stakeholders, and is a fundamental element of managing responsibility. Stakeholder engagement explicitly recognises the *mutuality* of interests and possible responses to any situation, issue, concern, problem or, indeed, opportunity. That is, a stakeholder engagement process goes two ways. Companies using stakeholder engagement recognise that not only will stakeholders sometimes need to change their attitudes, opinions, requests or demands, but also the company itself will sometimes have to do so as well.

Stakeholder engagement recognises the inherent power distribution between the company and its stakeholders and attempts to provide forums in which stakeholders can be heard in a setting where there is relative equality—and a willingness to shift position on the part of the company's management in order to be responsive to specific issues and concerns.

Stakeholder engagement then:

- Is inherently **interactive**

- Is based on **two-way communication** between companies and stakeholders

- Is based on processes of **dialogue** that allow for mutually derived solutions to problems and issues

- Requires **bringing all the relevant players** in a situation to the table in as equitable a way as feasible

- Provides a **voice** for stakeholders whose concerns might otherwise not be heard

- May **require change** on the company's as well as the stakeholders' side

4.8.2 Identify relevant stakeholders and stakeholder groups

Once the company has determined that it wishes to engage stakeholders, the next important task is to *identify* the relevant stakeholders. Stakeholders identified in a thorough process may or may not be simply the ones the company has traditionally taken into account.

Before going further, we must revisit the definition of stakeholder in more detail. The classic definition of a stakeholder is any group that can affect or is affected by an organisation's activities (Freeman 1984). Stakeholders are those individuals or groups that:

- Have taken some sort of risk by making an investment of some sort of 'capital' in the company. Investments by different stakeholders include:
    - Financial capital by investors/owners
    - Social capital investments by communities
    - Intellectual or human capital investments by employees and suppliers
    - Franchise (trust) capital by customers
    - Infrastructure and technological capital by suppliers and communities

- Can make claims on the company from a legal or moral perspective

- Have some sort of tie or relationship to the company. Ties or bonds to the company can include stakeholders who:
    - Identify with the company's mission
    - Are affected by some of the company's activities
    - Are concerned about an issue that the company's practices raise[2]

Most companies would acknowledge the importance of a certain set of stakeholders, called **primary stakeholders** (see, for example, Freeman 1984; Clarkson 1995; Waddock 2006). Primary stakeholders are those

---

2   For an elaboration of these ideas, see Waddock 2006.

groups without which a company cannot exist—and by virtue of being in business must, to some extent, serve. Primary stakeholders for all businesses are:

- Owners/investors
- Employees (and labour unions if the company is unionised)
- Customers
- Suppliers

Of course, each of these groups may be divided into different factions that have considerably different interests in or have taken substantially different risks with respect to the company. In addition, companies have groups of stakeholders that are considered to be secondary, those who are indirectly affected by or indirectly affect the activities of the firm. Typical **secondary stakeholder** groups include:

- Communities
- Governments in countries where the company has facilities, including:
  - Local governments
  - State or regional governments
  - National governments
  - International or multilateral decision-making bodies (e.g. the United Nations)

Increasingly, companies need to pay attention to groups that they once might have considered outside of their purview, including:

- Activist groups
- Non-governmental organisations (NGOs)

The other thing to recognise is that there will be **specific stakeholders** for each company to match its unique situation, as the leaders of ABB discovered when they began the stakeholder engagement process described in Box 4.5.

STAKEHOLDER ENGAGEMENT
ABB

ABB is a global corporation with headquarters in Switzerland operating in 100 countries and with 107,000 employees. The ABB Group has historically been known as a business-to-business (B2B) company serving its customers in manufacturing, process and consumer industries through utilities, the oil and gas sector, and infrastructure markets. Although the company is considered an industry leader in responsible environmental management, beginning in the late 1990s activists began criticising the company on both social and environmental grounds for its interest in supplying generators to the Three Gorges Dam project on the Yangtze River, China. This case examines ABB's process of extending its stakeholder engagement to civil society in response to these criticisms.

COMPANY HISTORY AND BACKGROUND

ABB was founded in 1987 with the merger of ASEA AB of Västerås, Sweden, and BBC Brown Boveri Ltd of Baden, Switzerland. It is a global engineering and technology company serving customers in electrical power generation, transmission and distribution; automation; oil, gas and petrochemicals; industrial products and contracting; and financial services. ABB employs 200,000 people in over 100 countries (www.abb.com).

CITIZENSHIP CHALLENGE

ABB took a leading role in the sustainable development movement following the 1992 Rio Convention. Given that ABB is primarily a business-to-business operation, however, the company had defined its primary stakeholders as customers, employees and shareholders. Having experienced considerable success in integrating environmental management systems across all business lines, ABB was caught off

Box 4.5 (continued opposite)

Sources: www.abb.com, accessed December 2006; annual reports web page (including sustainability reports): www02.abb.com/global/abbzh/abbzh251.nsf?OpenDatabase&db=/global/gad/ gad02077.nsf&v=e50a&e=us&&c=A5CA96EF8778E848C12570D2004855AE&m=6d4a&r=2, accessed December 2006; Social Policy Principles: www.abb.com/cawp/abbzh252/ 1d691c1f6d31d2b3c1257192003e1a31.aspx, accessed December 2006

guard by increasing environmental and social activism directed at it in the late 1990s. While ABB had committed itself to the environmental and economic sides of sustainable development, the social side remained under-developed.

Starting in 1997, the company began to receive attention from activists around its bid to source generators for the Three Gorges Dam project in China. This Three Gorges Dam, heralded as the largest in the history of the world, had drawn considerable negative attention from both environmental and social activists on the grounds of historical and ecological devastation, as well as for the displacement of nearly 1.9 million people. The activists' negative attention coincided with the announcement of the Global Compact by Kofi Annan at Davos in 1999 during a session that happened to be chaired by the ABB CEO, galvanising ABB's interest in developing its corporate citizenship profile. The impetus to develop ABB's social policy was further strengthened by the Dow Jones listing of ABB as first in its class in the 1999 Sustainability Index (DJSI).

THE STAKEHOLDER ENGAGEMENT PROCESS

In this environment of increasing activism and using the momentum generated by the positive attention of being the top-ranked company in DJSI, ABB began a three-step approach to stakeholder engagement. The first step was to form a task force of high-level corporate staff. Representatives from communications, investor relations and labour issues led the steering committee for this assessment. One of the task force's first actions was listing the company's social policy weaknesses.

The task force recognised that ABB had neither a social policy nor a group health and safety policy, which led to several recommendations to the CEO and board. The first recommendation was to join the Global Compact initiative as a means of supporting the social side of sustainability through a high-level commitment. The second recommendation was to continue developing social policies, first conducting a baseline study as a first action in order to understand ABB's pre-existing social programmes with an eye towards using this information to develop social policies.

Box 4.5 (from previous page; continued over)

In the course of conducting this research, ABB began actively recognising groups in civil society as important stakeholders, since the company had previously considered only employees, shareholders and stockholders to be their primary stakeholders. The task force sought to understand the company's social contributions in seven countries where operations were located (Brazil, China, Egypt, Poland, South Africa, Switzerland and the UK).

To conduct the research the task force added an outside sociologist who helped design an internal assessment methodology, using qualitative case studies. The steering committee developed a framework for implementing the research, which included cross-functional teams from the seven targeted countries used to assess the contributions of three main groups: (1) employees and families, (2) the local community, and (3) society at large (i.e. civil society). A local senior ABB manager supervised each national team and each country was responsible for commissioning local sociologists in order to provide professional guidance to their studies.

The initial research project took 4–5 months during 2000. The task force presented the results to the Sustainability Advisory Board. The board, formed in 1992, is composed of seven external members from business, NGOs, customers, shareholders, and the academic and science communities. It meets three times a year to provide continuous monitoring on ABB's sustainability matters. After the Advisory Board reviewed and approved the study, the major themes from the case studies formed the basis of an initial social policy draft for the company. This social policy comprised 13 principles, covering human rights, labour rights, suppliers, community involvement and business ethics. These principles (see below) were then benchmarked against international standards such as the Global Compact Principles, SA 8000, the OECD Guidelines for Multinational Enterprises, and the Global Sullivan Principles.

FOLLOW–UP

The social policy rough draft was then vetted in another round of stakeholder dialogues with 43 of ABB's local companies. Again, as with the development of the case studies, each of the local companies was

Box 4.5 (from previous page; continued opposite)

provided with a framework around which they could conduct dialogues and they were asked to seek stakeholder dialogue on the principles. Sample questions for the dialogue included: Were the principles suitable? Did they meet appropriate standards? Do they encompass all challenging situations encountered by ABB across the world? These discussions resulted in 25 reports and provided support for the principles. In addition to the positive response to the dialogues, stakeholders offered constructive feedback by identifying loopholes in the current construction of some principles and offering alternatives.

ABB'S SOCIAL POLICY (PRINCIPLES)

1. ABB in society
To contribute within the scope of our capabilities to improving economic, environmental and social conditions through open dialogue with stakeholders and through active participation in common effort.

2. Human rights
To support and respect the protection of internationally proclaimed human rights.

3. Children and young workers
To ensure that minors are properly protected; and as a fundamental principle, not to employ children or support the use of child labour, except as part of government-approved youth training schemes (such as work-experience programmes).

4. Freedom of engagement
To require that all employees enter into employment with the company of their own free will; and not to apply any coercion when engaging employees or support any form of forced or compulsory labour.

5. Health and safety
To provide a safe and healthy working environment at all sites and facilities and to take adequate steps to prevent accidents and injury to health arising out of the course of work by minimising, so far as is

Box 4.5 (from previous page; continued over)

reasonably practicable, the causes of hazards inherent in the working environment.

6. Employee consultation and communication

- To facilitate regular consultation with all employees to address areas of concern
- To respect the right of all personnel to form and join trade unions of their choice and to bargain collectively
- To ensure that representatives of personnel are not subject to discrimination and that such representatives have access to their members in the workplace
- To make sure, in any case of major lay-offs, that a social benefits and guidance plan is in place, and already known to employees or their official representatives

7. Equality of opportunity

To offer equality of opportunity to all employees and not to engage in or support discrimination in hiring, compensation, access to training, promotion, termination or retirement based on ethnic and national origin, caste, religion, disability, sex, age, sexual orientation, union membership, or political affiliation.

8. Mobbing and disciplinary practices

To counteract the use of mental or physical coercion, verbal abuse or corporal/hard-labour punishment; and not to allow behaviour, including gestures, language and physical contact, that is sexual, coercive, threatening, abusive or exploitative. To develop and maintain equitable procedures to deal with employee grievances, and disciplinary practices.

9. Working hours

To comply with applicable laws and industry standards on working hours, including overtime.

10. Compensation

- To ensure that wages paid meet or exceed the legal or industry minimum standards and are always sufficient to meet basic needs of personnel and to provide some discretionary income

Box 4.5 (from previous page; continued opposite)

- To ensure that wage and benefits composition are detailed clearly and regularly for workers, and that compensation is rendered in full compliance with all applicable laws and in a manner convenient to workers
- To ensure that labour-only contracting arrangements and false apprenticeship schemes are not used to avoid fulfilling ABB's obligations under applicable laws pertaining to labour and social security legislation and regulations

11. Suppliers
To establish and maintain appropriate procedures to evaluate and select major suppliers and subcontractors on their ability to meet the requirements of ABB's social policy and principles and to maintain reasonable evidence that these requirements are continuing to be met.

12. Community involvement
To promote and participate in community engagement activities that actively foster economic, environmental, social and educational development, as part of ABB's commitment to the communities where it operates.

13. Business ethics
To uphold the highest standards in business ethics and integrity and to support efforts of national and international authorities to establish and enforce high ethical standards for all businesses.

LESSONS LEARNED

- **Top-management commitment** is necessary to drive effective responsibility management as a corporate objective. By involving top managers from the beginning of the initial task force, ABB was able to cultivate this understanding at a senior management level
- **Having a clear research framework** determined in advance allowed companies to provide useful information about their operations and for headquarters analysis. Using external researchers to develop the guidelines for the qualitative baseline

Box 4.5 (from previous page; continued over)

study on community involvement provided subsidiaries with the appropriate amount of structure to gather relevant information

- **Iterative stakeholder engagement** offers opportunities to build trust and establish a climate for constructive feedback, change, and implementation of principles into practice

CHALLENGES ENCOUNTERED

- **Measurement** is one of the biggest challenges for ABB. The major question for ABB is what are the appropriate indicators and measures in the social dimensional of sustainability? As Michael Robertson, ABB Sustainability Affairs, pointed out, 'Some things are easier to measure than others; how do you begin to measure something like dialogue?'

- **Integration** of the social initiative through the corporation is another challenge. For example, in 2001 there were 600 employees working in the sustainability arena within ABB (at the country, factory, HQ staff and global business areas levels). This reality leads to the question stated by Robertson, 'How do we drive social performance through hierarchy and achieve what the mission statement says?'

Box 4.5 (from previous page)

4.8.3 Establish processes of engagement that bring key players to the table

Stakeholder engagement is best viewed as a long-term process with several important general goals and, typically, company-specific goals as well:

1. Building a long-term *relationship* with the stakeholders whose interests and investment in the company is important

2. Improving the *feedback* that a company gets about its activities from important constituencies, so that the company can . . .

3. Use the feedback in its *improvement and innovation* processes and systems to improve overall company performance

With these goals in mind, as well as the company-specific goals, companies developing stakeholder engagement processes have discovered that it is important that all of the relevant players be included in some way in the feedback system. They have realised that stakeholder engagement is not a 'once and done' one-time activity, but rather an ongoing series of exchanges, interaction and mutually defined responses.

There are several keys to making stakeholder engagement work, especially because different stakeholders will enter any conversation with their own perspectives, organisational cultures and goals:

1. Bring all of the relevant stakeholders into the system in some way that is appropriate to their interests and expectations

2. Develop ways to ensure that real *listening* is taking place on both sides. Work towards *dialogue*, which allows for the emergence of new ideas or what Buddhists call 'third-way thinking', which occurs when ideas brought by different parties are allowed to evolve into new solutions. Dialogue is evolutionary in that one idea builds on others, and ideas can frequently though not always be framed in win–win terms. Dialogue can be contrasted with discussion, where two opposing points of view are typically presented and each side tries to win the other over to its point of view without changing[3]

3. Find ways to ensure that relative amounts of power are equalised by parties coming from different types of organisation and with different resource bases within the context of the stakeholder engagement

4. Develop a common vision of what the group is to accomplish together

---

3   This point is dramatically made in Peter Senge's 1990 seminal book *The Fifth Discipline* (updated edition 2006).

5. Be judicious in how much commitment and interaction is expected of stakeholders, recognising that they have their own commitments and interests

6. Be respectful of stakeholders' time, energy and commitment, and, when promises for change are made, carry them out

4.8.4 Communication channels

Keeping the goals described above and the company-specific goals in mind, companies next need to establish stakeholder engagement channels that are unique to their specific cultures, industries and situations. For example, stakeholder engagement can occur through feedback sessions, focused group meetings, web-based communication channels, 'town' or company-based meetings, informal get-togethers in which information is shared, or other means. Cisco Systems is one company that has developed technologically sophisticated means to implement its inspirational vision, management commitment and stakeholder engagement processes (see Box 4.6).

The key to developing ongoing relationships with stakeholders is setting up *appropriate* communication channels, as Cisco Systems recognises. Many companies engage with various stakeholders all the time, but many do not think of that engagement as part of an interactive dialogue that helps provide important feedback and new information about possible issues and concerns to the company. Raising awareness of the need to actively *engage* with stakeholders is a first step, and then setting up specific channels through which this engagement occurs is the second step. The third step is taking what has been learned and putting it into appropriate actions that either modify the way the company has been acting or works with stakeholders to explain what is happening.

Not all stakeholders necessarily need to or should have input on every decision; it is clear that management needs to reserve some decisions. Management can be better informed about most of its decisions, however, if it takes into account the interests, risks and needs of its different constituencies before making the decision. These interests, risks and needs can best be learned from the stakeholders themselves by engaging with them interactively in dialogue.

CISCO SYSTEMS
VISIONARY LEADERS AND STAKEHOLDER ENGAGEMENT

Called by *Business Week* an 'unabashed evangelist for radical changes in management', Cisco Systems CEO John T. Chambers has put his vision or a new, progressive business model into practice in the company. Taking the perspective that 'clicks-and-mortar will become the only means of survival', Chambers has built Cisco Systems into the world's most internet-centric big company, according to *Fast Company* magazine. Here is one company in which personal and organisational vision are unified.

Cisco's vision is that the internet will transform the way people work, live, play and learn. Today change is happening faster than ever before, and Cisco helps companies turn that change into a competitive advantage, by helping them become agile. How? With expertise, a strong network of partners, and superior technology including intelligent network services and scalable architectures. Cisco is the worldwide leader in networking for the internet (www.cisco. com/warp/public/779/largeent/why_cisco/vision.html).

With a will to put jobs wherever the right infrastructure, educated workforce and supportive government exist, Chambers bills the company as the business network solution. Aiming to provide network resources enterprise-wide, Cisco Systems provides a comprehensive line of networking products. The company's mission is nothing less than to 'shape the future of the internet by creating unprecedented value and opportunity for our customers, employees, investors, and ecosystem partners'.

Cisco has sales offices in about 115 countries, using direct sales, distributors, value-added resellers and system integrators to reach its customers, who are large complex 'enterprises' (large corporations, governments and institutions where networking capability is needed),

Box 4.6 (continued over)

Sources: Waddock 2006; www.cisco.com/warp/public/779/largeent/why_cisco/vision.html; various parts of the Cisco website; Byrne 2000; Muoio 2000; www.cisco.com/web/learning/netacad/index.html, accessed December 2006; www.cisco.com/warp/public/779/edu/academy/overview/fast_facts.html, accessed August 2004; Eizengerg *et al.* 2001; updates are from www.conference-board.org/utilities/pressDetail.cfm?press_ID=2235

service providers, and small and medium-sized businesses. Founded in 1986, the company has grown dramatically and is now the market leader in most of the market segments in which it is active. With expected annual revenues of over US$22 billion in 2004, the company has become one of the largest companies in the world.

Cisco's unique strategy is built on establishing excellent—and online—relationships with its primary stakeholders. It has built an internal network structure that allows its stakeholders instant access to the company and its resources from anywhere around the world. For customers, Cisco has the IPC, Internetworking Product Centre, which allows customers to order online and have access to technical support, speeding processing of orders and deliveries. Potential customers can log on to the CCO, Cisco Connection Online, to get instant access to detailed corporate information, products and services.

Suppliers are networked through the CSC, Cisco Supplier Connection, which allows direct access to Cisco's materials resource planning system and enables suppliers to monitor orders and ship automatically. Partners are linked through the PICA, the Partner-Initiated Customer Access, which provides resources for sales initiatives, and employees are connected via the CEC, Cisco's Employee Connection, an intranet that is intended to improve productivity (Eizengerg *et al.* 2001).

But it isn't just size or its 80% market share that makes Cisco a visionary company. Chambers is clear about the type of organisation his vision implies. 'The reason people stay at a company is that it's a great place to work. It's like playing on a great sports team. Really good players want to be around other really good players. Secondly, people like to work for good leadership. So creating a culture of leaders that people like is key. And the third is, are you working for a higher purpose than an IPO or a paycheck? Our higher purpose is to change the way the world works, lives, and plays' (Byrne 2000).

To live up to these standards, Cisco applies its corporate citizenship very broadly to its customer and ally relationships, and has also implemented a number of strategically important community- and education-oriented programmes. For example Cisco deploys

Box 4.6 (from previous page; continued opposite)

employee volunteers in local communities into many local projects with corporate support. More important to its mission as a network services provider, the company has established the Cisco Community and Educational Technical Advocates (CETA) programme, which integrates technical expertise and assistance into Cisco technology grants given to educational institutions.

Most important of all, Cisco has established a programme that will ensure a trained base of employees in the future, while providing much-needed help to many school systems, in its Networking Academy Program. The Academies teach high-school and college students how to design, build and maintain computer networks, with a curriculum that ranges from basic networking skills to advanced troubleshooting tools.

Organised as an innovative public–private partnership, the Academies provide 280 hours of web-based, hands-on curriculum in 84 countries and all 50 of the United States. Some 81,000 students are estimated to be enrolled in the 5,040 Academies; more than 10,000 had graduated by the summer of 2000. Cisco's Chambers has clearly discovered a way to 'do well and do good'. Cisco's initial US$20 million investment in the Academies promises to yield long-term benefits not only to graduates of the programme, who will have useful and needed skills, but also to the company itself and to the schools that benefit from getting resources essential to educating tomorrow's workforce.

In 2003, Cisco was granted the US Department of Commerce's Ron Brown Award for its achievements in employee and community relations, signifying national recognition of its accomplishments.

Box 4.6 (from previous page)

Dialogue, as noted above, involves interaction and mutuality, hence two-way communication. Communication channels need to be appropriate for the specific stakeholder, the functional area most involved with that stakeholder, and for the company as a whole. For example, companies concerned about customer relationships might set up focused group interviews or customer feedback sessions where marketing, production and quality managers can interact with and learn from customers about their views of the company's products or services, and where they can also share their own perspectives. Companies' community relations officers, and sometimes environmental affairs managers, sometimes hold interactive meetings with community representatives to listen to community-based concerns, issues and opportunities for engagement.

Some companies use their websites creatively to engage their stakeholders. One company that is explicitly focused on stakeholder engagement is Unilever, as Box 4.7 discusses.

4.9 Communicate, communicate, communicate . . . with stakeholders

The Unilever case in Box 4.7 illustrates not only the importance of developing engagement processes with stakeholders, but also just how important it is to communicate constantly and interactively with those stakeholders on an ongoing basis to ensure that both sides are heard. Companies that wish to be in an engaged relationship with their important stakeholders need to find ways to communicate what they are doing openly and transparently. Increasingly, members of the societies in which companies operate are expecting them to be accountable for their impacts. Such accountability requires transparency of action, behaviour, decisions and results to the relevant stakeholders. As we will see in the Chapter 7, it is important to measure how well the company is achieving its responsibility goals and objectives.

It is equally important that the company communicates openly and regularly with its employees and key stakeholders in forums geared to

UNILEVER STAKEHOLDER ENGAGEMENT

Unilever Corporation, the global consumer products company, has developed an extensive and explicit strategy for engaging with its stakeholders. The company explicitly recognises that 'We operate in increasingly complex yet interconnected societies. We believe we can contribute most effectively by being open and working in partnership with our stakeholders.'

To operationalise its stakeholder engagement processes, the company consults widely with a diverse array of stakeholders as a means of learning from them what their concerns are. These stakeholder groups include employees, customers, consumers, business partners, investors, governments and regulators. Different processes are used with different stakeholder groups. For example, the company undertakes formal customer/consumer research, opinion surveys and makes contributions to public policy debates and community meetings. It also engages in informal dialogues with NGOs when feasible, specifically starting a programme in 2003 of informal meetings with small groups of stakeholders on topics of mutual interest, where senior Unilever executives participate actively.

In addition the company has established working relationships with a variety of UN agencies and NGOs, including UNICEF, the World Health Organisation, the Red Cross/Crescent and Oxfam, and works with governments and non-profit organisations on issues of joint concern. A member of the UN Global Compact, Unilever is also active in that organisation's social dialogue processes, and is an active member of numerous organisations concerned with business responsibility and ethics, such as Ethos in Brazil, Business for Social Responsibility in the USA, and CSR Europe.

To test whether its participation with stakeholders had any impact, Unilever conducted an independent survey in 2002 among 38 leading corporate responsibility and sustainable development opinion leaders in the US and Europe. The results were somewhat mixed, indicating a way to go, but on the whole the opinion leaders believed that Unilever manages its responsibilities well . . . though it needs to communicate even better with stakeholders. Results of the survey were fed back into the stakeholder engagement process so that it could be improved.

Box 4.7

Sources: www.unilever.com/ourvalues; 'Environmental Performance Report 2003', www.unilever.com/Images/2003%20Environmental%20Performance%20report_tcm13-5056.pdf, accessed February 2007

interacting with each group. Thus, employee communication channels will mostly likely be internal forums. Companies can communicate via newsletters, internal email systems, employee focus groups and town meetings, and in other creative ways.

Unique and different forums can be created on a periodic basis with worker representatives, community representatives and governmental officials at different levels. Customer forums can provide important feedback about the company's products and services, while supplier and distributor forums can help both partners improve the infrastructure that connects the two companies as well as the productivity of the interactions.

Communications with authorities, such as governments and regulators, are important, too, as are ways of dealing with critical audiences, such as some NGOs or activist organisations. Unilever's strategy illustrates a balanced, forward-looking and comprehensive approach to stakeholder engagement.

5

Integration

Integration in TRM means that companies are paying close attention to how well the responsibility vision, values and stakeholder engagement processes they have developed are actually integrated into strategies and operating practices. This integration process involves three major components: integration into company strategies for achieving the corporate vision and purposes; integration into employee policies and practices, because, after all, it is the employee who actually accomplishes the work of the organisation; and integration into functional areas that deal with other stakeholders and into management systems, in particular the reward system.

5.1 Defining strategy: what business are we in?

In the last chapter, we explored the importance of establishing the company's inspirational vision and accompanying core values. Equally important is determining the specific strategic goals and direction that the company will use to achieve the vision and the functional strategies that support the overall strategy.

Company strategy provides needed direction and a set of goals to strive for. Strategy at the corporate level involves answering the important strategic question: What business(es) are we in?

Moving the strategic question down to the business level, the company asks: How do we compete?

Addressing the values question, as noted earlier, requires asking: What do we stand for?

Answering these questions effectively involves focusing on how the company's values are integrated into its functional and operating strategies: that is, the practices (policies, procedures and processes) that a company develops to achieve its goals. After all, it is through operating practices and stakeholder relationships that a company's actions and decisions have an impact on its stakeholders.

In today's dynamic and rapidly evolving world, answering the 'what business are we in?' and even the 'what do we stand for?' questions does not always provide enough guidance to managers. Today's managers' lives are fraught with the complexities of dealing with multiple stakeholders who bring different demands and concerns to their attention. The purpose, after all, of specifying a strategy is to provide direction and guidance to the organisation. Strategy, especially when widely shared throughout the company, has the capacity to inform everyone in the company about what the company is going to do (i.e. the goals and objectives) and *how* it will be done.

In responsibility management approaches, the answers to this question also involve clearly linking the *way* a company competes to the core values and the responsibility vision. Thus, the development of strategy explicitly incorporates vision and values into the means by which goals are achieved. To do this well means expanding the company's traditional focus beyond simply 'maximising shareholder wealth', as has been noted in the earlier chapters.

5.2 Beyond customers to multiple stakeholders

Quality management focuses on making the end customer happy, by producing a product that satisfies that individual whose satisfaction would translate into future business. Taking a TRM approach means expanding the focus to include other stakeholders affected by the company's actions. The reason for this expansion of managerial horizons is clear. In the end, firm performance is affected not only by satisfying customers who actually buy a company's products or services, but also by satisfying those stakeholders who set government policies, influence public opinion and organisational reputation, produce the company's products and services, and influence the productivity of the firm. All of this has to do with the externally perceived legitimacy of the firm as an actor in society. In an era when large multinational corporations' power and control of resources is increasingly in question, the underlying issue of legitimacy—or what some call the licence to operate—is a critically important one that executives need to address. One way of dealing with this fundamental issue is by integrating the concerns of multiple stakeholders into the business model.

To take into account the multiple demands of these stakeholders, a company's management, operating in its own best interests, and based on bottom-line considerations, needs to broaden consideration of which stakeholders it is trying to satisfy through its responsibility management systems. Companies need to take the interests and needs of multiple stakeholders into account when they shape their internal practices, and particularly when they begin thinking about how the corporate vision, values and purpose will affect strategies, operating practices and behaviours. Stakeholders whose interests and concerns need consideration do, of course, include final customers. But most companies also need to include government representatives, employees, unions, NGOs and community leaders, among others, as important stakeholders specific to the company and its industry, as well as where it has operations (i.e. all of the primary and secondary stakeholders discussed in the previous chapters).

What will help a firm enjoy a good and sustainable market? In most markets today, economic and competitive sustainability means continually changing, updating and improving the product or service, as well as all the systems employed to design, develop, produce and deliver the product or service. Increasingly, what is meant by 'quality' includes gaining the confidence of customers and other stakeholders about the *manner* by which a firm produces its products, as well as the product characteristics. For example, not only do today's customers care about product price and physical characteristics; they also want to be sure that forced or child labour was not used in the product's production, and that workers were paid at least (local) minimum wage and not cheated out of their rightful earnings. Customers and other stakeholders, such as NGOs, activists, governmental officials and some owners increasingly care about a company's internal practices, especially those that affect employees, such as:

- Labour standards and working conditions
- Human rights
- Environmental sustainability
- Corporate integrity, transparency and accountability

Stakeholders care, that is, about a company's responsibility management systems and how different stakeholders, particularly employees, are treated as the company translates its strategies into the practices that enable a company to deliver its goods. They care about the *integration* of the responsibility management system into practice.

Of course, this view expands the definition of product and creates a much more demanding and complex world for managers. Whether they like it or not, managers have to contend with the new reality that multiple stakeholders with different types of demand put significant pressures on the integrity and responsibility of their practices. Generally speaking, in the past producing a product that was well priced and well made in the eyes of the final customer was all that a firm needed to do to be successful. Now companies face a raft of other concerns.

Many of these questions focus on how well employees, even in the extended supply chain, are treated. For example, NGOs can ask whether suppliers are able to enforce child labour requirements, in the light of poor worker documentation. Will union workers accept requirements in a company's code of conduct concerning working hours? Environmental issues also are raised. For example, will NGOs point out that the product production, which was carried out by a distant sub-component supplier, polluted local water supplies? These and myriad other questions face the modern organisation. And these considerations cannot be ignored, because in the end their answers and the implications of their answers for the management of responsibility in the organisation help determine the company's very success in markets increasingly concerned with labour conditions, the environment, human rights and company (and broader system) integrity. Box 5.1 explains how to begin thinking about some of these considerations and the hidden costs associated with them.[1]

5.3 Integrating responsibility management into strategy and systems

Taking quality management and extending it to responsibility management does not require a great leap of the imagination. Let us consider the apparel and footwear sectors. If we look at these sectors historically, the largest firms began to take working conditions and labour practices into account as part of their responsibilities in the early 1990s. At that time (and continuing today) many companies were under fire from sweatshop, child labour and environmental activists. The activists and the media subjected companies where problems were uncovered to considerable negative publicity, consumer boycotts and other reputational damage that cost customers and made recruitment of employees more difficult.

---

1 Some of the thinking in this section is based on Mamic 2004, and the underlying study, also by Mamic (2003).

THE HIDDEN COST OF VARIABILITY

One of the primary causes of poor quality, in the view of W. Edwards Deming and other scholars, is the lack of stability in processes—the costs to quality caused by shifting outcomes and unpredictability. Let us extend this thinking to suppliers. Whereas cost considerations often dictate shopping for the lowest possible cost for labour or parts, the hidden costs of such an approach are often overlooked. Companies typically face unaccounted for set-up charges in working with new suppliers. These costs include administrative burden, loss of volume discounts, untrained workers, poor productivity and, perhaps most importantly, the lack of trust and reliability that comes with an ever-changing selection of contributors.

We can find similar hidden costs with regard to the management of responsibility—as well as product quality—in modern globalised supply chains. With cost a driving factor in such chains, purchasing departments typically have to shop around for the lowest possible price for 'reliable' output. Such costs are often quite clearly demonstrated. If one supplier charges US$2.25 a shirt for an order of 10,000 and another supplier charges US$1.75 for an item of the same quality with the same delivery terms, the saving is clearly US$5,000. Or is it? Hidden costs may be much more difficult to measure but be of even greater importance.

What would be the cost of having the supplier provide 10,000 shirts tainted with benzene? Or of having the supplier suffer a wildcat strike due to unrecompensed overtime that delays production by two months? What would be the reputational cost of having either of these events broadcast on BBC, CNN or StarTV as examples of uncontrolled and irresponsible globalisation? Such questions need to be considered when a company considers what degree of commitment it will make to responsibility management. Although such costs can seldom be boiled down to a simple comparison of ROI (returns on investment), they are very real.

Box 5.1

To address the concerns raised by critics, many of the footwear and apparel firms adopted codes of conduct that outlined what was and what was not acceptable behaviour throughout their supply chains. These codes of conduct were then distributed as part of purchase contracts to suppliers. The suppliers were then responsible for ensuring compliance with the new codes of conduct. This rather limited approach to responsibility management was based on expanding the contractual obligations of suppliers to cover labour practices, human rights and related issues. Because the obligations were quite specific, they required minimal involvement of the legal, purchasing and perhaps communications and public relations departments of the buyers and little real integration of the standards into the company's operating policies and practices.

This limited approach to responsibility management lasted through much of the 1990s. By 1997 several very prominent cases of what the public considered unacceptable practice in the production chains of the larger apparel and footwear manufacturers, as well as other companies with long supply chains in developing nations had come to light. These practices generated considerable unfavourable attention for the companies concerned. As a result, an increasing number of apparel and footwear brands began explicitly accepting responsibility for the labour and environmental practices in their supply chains. In addition to the changes that these new responsibilities required in corporate vision— vision that had to shift prior to any wide-scale shift in actual practice—the new focus had dramatic implications for the integration of responsibility into the daily management systems and processes across the organisations of the sector.

Most codes of conduct in the apparel business, for example, prohibit child and forced labour, as well as discrimination, and require suppliers to allow workers the right to associate freely and bargain collectively. Accepting responsibility for working conditions means that these companies are in fact working with hundreds of suppliers to improve conditions. These shifts in who is responsible for working conditions represent an enormous undertaking. Especially in the light of continually shifting supplier relationships, ensuring responsible practice is a never-ending task. Responsibility management touches on many if not most activities and processes in supply chains such as those in the apparel industry.

Although we cannot detail all aspects of how responsibility management is being integrated in apparel companies, a few illustrations may be helpful. Below we explain some of the shifts needed to accommodate responsibility management within supply chains in the areas of purchasing, quality assurance and legal compliance.

5.3.1 Purchasing

In the apparel sector, contracts are issued on the basis of individual job orders, rather than by establishing a business partnership basis that exists over a period of time.[2] Purchasing is the primary lever of change when a company is dealing with suppliers. When companies accepted responsibility for the supply chain, the role of purchasing officers and departments had to change away from their traditional targeting of the lowest price for the needed levels of quality and delivery. New goals included achieving the price and quality objectives while simultaneously ensuring compliance with corporate responsibility objectives set in codes of conduct. This shift created the need to develop compliance feedback information systems that provide purchasing teams with the information necessary to make decisions that include responsibility-related performance. Also, since people tend to do what they are rewarded for, it has meant that pay and other rewards need to be linked to compliance. Thus, of course, performance appraisal systems needed to be adjusted to these new demands and requirements.

---

2   This is not to say that buyers and suppliers do not develop long-term relationships in the apparel sector. Many do. Rather, even with such relationships lasting years the contractual basis is still, typically, short-term contracts for jobs done. At the same time, suppliers tend to provide product to various buyers, seldom dedicating more than 20% of their production to any one buyer. As such, suppliers spread the risk of a fall-off in business among a variety of customers and reduce the leverage of any one buyer to demand special conditions of production.

5.3.2 Quality assurance

Most companies' compliance departments are stretched too thin to visit each factory often enough to ensure compliance. As a result, the job of regular review has fallen in many cases to quality assurance (QA) personnel. QA team members are in factories regularly, examining products before they are authorised for shipment—and they are typically the only buyer group visiting supplier sites on a regular basis. Expanding their responsibilities to include responsibility issues is a major change because QA personnel have not typically been trained, for example, to assess fire safety systems, the use of toxic materials or personnel protection equipment, much less labour practices or payroll systems. Yet, given their regular presence in suppliers, many firms have found that QA can be the front line for responsibility management system and compliance assurance, providing continuous pressure on suppliers to comply with codes of conduct.

5.3.3 Legal departments

Globalisation of supply chains and the outsourcing of production initially moved the responsibility for labour and environmental practices further down the production chain, making it the responsibility of those firms actually producing the goods for the buyer, rather than the buyer or brand itself. As codes of conduct have become common, and as NGOs, student activists and others have demanded increased responsibility of buyer firms, legal departments have seen the range of their concerns grow. For example, the contractual obligations established when supplying goods to many universities often now include the requirement that the branding company make certain guarantees about how the goods were produced. Many of these production activities go on outside of what have traditionally been considered the buying organisation's boundaries. To further complicate matters, the US government and the European Union are both examining establishing similar requirements on buyers.

These examples are but the tip of an iceberg of the many changes in systems that are actually needed as companies struggle to develop and implement responsibility management as a source of competitive advantage and to avoid being targets of corporate critics. In what follows we will present some general guidelines to help you think through a systemic approach to integrating responsibility management systems.

5.4 Integrating responsibility management

Every firm's situation is, of course, unique. Thus, it is not possible to say exactly what the impact of setting responsibility objectives and then really attempting to achieve them mean for a specific firm. As one example, however, we can consider what took place with a designer in the sports apparel sector. Interviewed in Vietnam, he discussed how achieving environmental objectives meant designers were no longer free to develop products using whatever materials they thought appropriate. With the code of conduct in place, the company now has to consider the impact of chosen materials on the environment.

This change seemed somehow immediately understandable to him. What he had not expected or understood—until he travelled to one of his firm's large suppliers in Vietnam—was the impact that his job could have on the labour practices at the factory level. He explained how, with deadline pressures cutting into his team's design window, he ordered a large number of samples to be developed by the factory half a world away. The cost of the rush order was acceptable given the project's budget. Because of unexpected delays earlier in design, delays that in retrospect he agreed could have been avoided, the only time that could be squeezed was the time available for testing. It was only when he travelled to Asia to visit the factory that he found out the implications of this decision to rush the testing process. The benefits of the decision, which had appeared so clear cut at headquarters, meant that hundreds of workers had to put in well over the maximum of 60 hours of work per week allowed by the company's code to finish the job on schedule.

As mentioned, it is not possible to fully detail here what processes have to change in the organisation, what job requirements need to shift, what information systems supporting these changes are required and what the implications of these changes will be. Integrating responsibility into the organisation is contingent on many factors unique to each situation. These factors include:

- The level of responsibility that the firm intends to adopt

- The nature of its business

- The current state of its various management systems

- The quality and extent of its supplier relationships

- The culture and country in which suppliers are located

- A multiplicity of other factors specific to the firm

What is clear is that responsibility management approaches must be both systemic and holistic if they are to be effective. Once the decision is made to manage responsibility, the company needs to pay close attention to all of the systems that support its productive processes, as well as its employees, customers, communities, owners, suppliers and other stakeholders.

In taking a holistic approach, responsibility management is once again mirroring earlier changes wrought by quality management. Firms adopting total quality systems needed to ask themselves 'How do we satisfy our customers?' rather than 'How do we make this product?' They still needed to consider the second question, but only after the first had been answered. Similarly, companies today need to be able to answer the question, 'How do we meet the needs or demands of all of our stakeholders and remain profitable?' not just 'How do we maximise profits for our shareholders?'

Integrating responsibility into the organisation, in other words, is the *process* of ensuring achievement of a firm's responsibility vision through organisation-wide efforts; it requires a firm to ask many questions and also stay focused on profitability. In addition to answering the question of *what* it wants to achieve, the firm needs to ask the primary *how* question: How do our activities have an impact on our responsibility performance?

Typically, as they did with initial efforts to improve quality, companies first look down the chain, all the way to the suppliers and their actions. The challenge with responsibility management is to look wider and further along the supply chain than is necessary with quality management. Some typical questions might be:

- How do our purchasing systems affect supplier actions?

- How do our human resource policies stand up in terms of their responsibility?

- What are our hiring, promotion, recruitment and lay-off policies?

- What kinds of working condition exist within our own operations and those of our suppliers?

- What will have to change in our marketing plan to take into account changes in our strategic objectives brought about by a new vision of responsibility?

- How do we work with the communities where we have facilities?

- What kind of environmental impacts do our operations have? How can we mitigate negative impacts? Are there ways to move towards sustainability?

- Do our designers take environmental impacts into account in their designs?

What is clear from this overview of different functional areas and some focusing questions is that integration begins with an open and questioning mind, and proceeds to a holistic management approach to improvement and process redesign. Some examples of the functional areas and related practices that need consideration in responsibility management are illustrated in Table 5.1.

Determining how to integrate responsibility means that leaders need to take a holistic or systemic approach that takes all of a company's practices and impacts into consideration. Thus, integration of responsibility management can mean rethinking how the company relates to all of its

FUNCTIONAL AREA	PRACTICES: PROCESSES AND POLICIES
Human resources	• Hiring, recruitment, retention policies • Appraisal, assessment, performance review • Dismissal and lay-off policies • Promotion • Training and development programmes • Working conditions, safety • Management style, employee empowerment • Implementation of code of conduct
Marketing	• Product design • Public relations • Product quality, impacts, safety • Advertising and promotional strategies • Customer relationships
Finance	• Sources and uses of capital • Integrity of financing sources • Distribution process for using financing
Accounting and control	• Responsibility measurement system • Multiple (triple)-bottom-line assessment • Integrity, transparency, accountability
Operations	• Production processes • Labour and working standards • Lighting • Safety systems
Supplier relationships	• Contractual obligations • Code of conduct implementation • Environmental management systems • Employee/labour requirements and conditions

TABLE 5.1 Some functions and processes affected by TRM
(continued over)

FUNCTIONAL AREA	PRACTICES: PROCESSES AND POLICIES
Management information systems	● Control and dissemination of key information ● Use of information gathered ● Employee communication system ● External communication system
Environmental management system	● Waste disposal, pollution control ● Environmental, health and safety practices ● Packaging and production considerations ● Resource re-use, reduction, recycling
Community relations	● Neighbour-of-choice practices ● Philanthropic strategy ● Volunteering and community-building actions

TABLE 5.1 (from previous page)

internal and external stakeholders, how effective and efficient its resource use, production processes and distribution systems are, as well as how well the company is living up to its stated values. Further, the company's values as operationalised in its stakeholder-related practices need to be consistent with the growing array of external standards and principles—foundation values—that stakeholders expect companies to meet. The whole organisation is thus affected by TRM. When responsibility management is taken seriously, the outcome is likely to be better overall management and a more productive, therefore more profitable, company, though it is clear that some costs will be incurred in implementing new systems and not all of those new systems will in fact 'pay off' in profitability terms.

All of this is not to say that it is easy to implement TRM systems. The very complexity of expanding the definition of which stakeholders matter and what needs to be attended to works against simplicity. Although expanding responsibility for responsibility beyond a compliance team to include any and all parts of the organisation that impact on the achievement of responsibility objectives is potentially an enormous task, it is clear that it is also the new business imperative. Companies that fail to attend to their stakeholder relationships and the responsibility of their practices will increasingly find themselves the subjects of negative media and internet reports, customer boycotts, disinvestment by unsatisfied socially conscious investors, not to mention low employee morale and productivity.

5.5 Integration of responsibility management into the supply chain

One of the stickier areas for integration of responsibility management systems in multinational companies is in the increasingly long supply chains that many of these companies have established in the effort to be globally competitive and achieve low-cost production. A study by the International Labour Organisation[3] of global supply chains focused on how leading firms, which are under the greatest pressures to improve labour practices in their suppliers, have progressed from denying responsibility for conditions in supplier factories to embracing this responsibility. Indeed, they are rolling up their sleeves and taking on board the challenge of improving labour, human rights and environmental practices, as well as the overall integrity of their systems through implementation of strict codes of conduct and responsibility standards.

Taking the step to accept responsibility beyond what is typically seen as the borders of the firm is not an easy decision, as must be obvious. It is one thing to say 'We make our suppliers sign a code of conduct that we expect them to follow.' It is entirely another thing to say 'We expect our suppliers to follow our code. We work with them to help them meet the code. We check to ensure they do, and if they don't then we don't work with them any longer.' Yet this is exactly what the companies studied are doing today.

3   Reported in Waddock *et al.* 2002 and Waddock and Bodwell 2002. For additional examples see also Hartman *et al.* 2001 and Mamic 2003.

Creating a code of conduct is challenging, but not nearly as challenging as taking this second step, accepting responsibility down the chain and introducing all the management systems necessary to make it possible. The firms who have gone through this process have realised that taking this second step requires an organisation-wide approach, not a narrow consideration of purchasing and compliance functions. Really implementing the code, truly taking responsibility for labour practices in distant suppliers, requires a broad-based consideration of what affects the ability to meet the responsibility goals of the organisation and making sure that things are done right.

Effective responsibility management thus requires the same sort of dedication and organisational commitment that firms had to give during the quality revolution of the 1980s and early 1990s. If *The Economist* (2001) is correct that 'The next big thing in brands is social responsibility', then implementing TRM is going to require its own organisational revolution, very much like what was experienced in the 1980s with the quality revolution. And it is going to require the same type of broad level of consideration that quality received, leading to what we have conceptualised as a type of total responsibility management.

As with effective quality management, effective responsibility management requires setting clear goals. How many defects do you want per million may be a quality issue. With responsibility the objectives are different but require the same systematic consideration of what it takes to get there. How do we eliminate child labour from our suppliers? How do we ensure that discrimination is not taking place? Or abuse? Or workers are not working past the limits on overtime set by the company or local governments?

With issues such as those noted above, limiting responsibility management to the compliance or audit teams, or even to these as well as to the purchasing group, is not a feasible alternative. People throughout the organisation have an effect on the ability of a firm and its suppliers to meet international labour standards, national labour, human rights or environmental regulations, or the firm's own code of conduct. Thus, the whole *system* and all the functions supporting it need attention, not just strict issues of compliance.

Managing responsibility for what takes place down through supply chains means changing systems for quality, production, measurement, training and personnel, among other factors. It is a huge job . . . just ask Adidas, The Gap, Ikea, Nike, Unilever, and all the other big brand-name companies who have moved in this direction under the pressure of activists, consumers, labour unions and employees. They all, to one degree or another, have begun this process of managing responsibility. And managing responsibility, as with quality management, is a process that will never end. There will always be new suppliers, new standards, higher goals, crises and changes in markets that need renewed attention. The case of Novo's Human Rights Framework (Box 5.2) shows how one company has begun the long-term process of integrating foundation values and its own standards into its operating practices.

5.6 Some guiding questions for developing TRM

Many companies need to know how to begin developing responsibility management approaches. Below we present some guiding questions for managing responsibility—questions that can potentially help companies to gain the competitive edge that managing responsibility provides. Company executives should first try to undertake a diagnostic process that helps them determine whether their current practices meet stakeholder expectations, both internally and externally. The following questions can be helpful in that diagnostic process:

- Is there a *gap* between our stated responsibility vision, values and goals and the way we actually operate day to day? Or in our impact on the different stakeholders on whom we depend for our existence? Where is this gap evident?
  - In terms of labour standards and practices?
  - In the way we treat people?
  - In our supplier relationships?

INTEGRATION INTO EMPLOYEE RELATIONSHIPS
NOVO'S HUMAN RIGHTS FRAMEWORK

Demands arising from the business environment, such as the customer service and total quality movements in the 1960s and 1970s, provided companies with an opportunity evaluate their overall vision. Likewise, the increase in consumer, civil-society and governmental demands for corporate accountability regarding labour, community and the environment encouraged some firms to re-evaluate their purpose to incorporate these ideals. The Novo Group has developed a process for choosing human rights as the platform to guide their economic, social and environmental performance. Novo's selection of the human rights platform exemplifies critical aspects of the TRM vision setting and strategic planning processes.

COMPANY HISTORY AND BACKGROUND

The Novo Group is a family of independent companies with a common history and shared values. All Novo Group companies share and benefit from the governance principles stated in the Novo Group Charter. Novo Nordisk A/S is a global niche pharmaceutical company with biotechnology expertise focusing on diabetes care, haemophilia, and products for growth disorders and hormone replacement therapy. Novozymes A/S is a biotechnology-based company developing, producing and selling enzymes for industrial use to the three market segments: technical, food and animal feed. Novo A/S is an investment and holding company owned 100% by the Novo Nordisk Foundation with the purpose of managing the Novo Nordisk Foundation's funds and investment in companies in and outside the bio-industrial and biopharmaceutical area (www.novonordisk.com)

FROM ENVIRONMENTAL MANAGEMENT AND HUMAN RESOURCES TO HUMAN RIGHTS

Starting 20 years ago Novo began examining environmental issues as they moved to the top of the agenda along with strengthened

Box 5.2 (continued opposite)

Source: Novo Nordisk Foundation: www.novonordisk.com/about_us/corporate_governance/foundation.asp, accessed December 2006; Novo Group A/S (Holding Company): www.novo.dk, accessed December 2006; Novo Nordisk home page: www.novonordisk.com, accessed December 2006; Novozymes: www.novozymes.com/en

regulatory laws in Denmark. In the mid-1990s as the social agenda emerged, Novo put together an internal group to gain an understanding of what corporate social responsibility (CSR) meant to their business and the best ways to change their businesses to incorporate these concerns. In 1997 Novo began working with an external consultant to determine its own corporate social responsibility vision that would guide the company's future community, environmental and economic initiatives.

At that time the company looked at social responsibility issues, such as employee welfare, from a human resources viewpoint. In its first step of assessing its responsibility vision—a key aspect of TRM— Novo hired a consultant to conduct an analysis of the human resource approach to social responsibility with employees and external stakeholders. A SWOT analysis was carried out, presenting strengths, weaknesses, opportunities and threats to the firm's responsibility goals and practices. After this stakeholder engagement process, the consulting report recommended that the company adopt a broader human rights platform as its social responsibility orientation.

The human rights platform offered several benefits to the company. Because Novo is a multinational company that operates with affiliates in 79 countries and sells its products in 179 countries, taking the UN human rights approach endorsed by the largest international organisations in the world seemed appropriate. The UN Declaration on Human Rights and the Environment is the world's most prominent expression of universally recognised values. Novo made a strong commitment to incorporate the broadest and most accepted international standards as a central tenet of its responsibility management vision. Novo's selection of human rights became the underpinning of its policies. This approach was strengthened by developments that have taken place in support of the Declaration; as it is based on commitments to international agreements, the UN has documented each element in detailed conventions that describe specifically what the agreements mean in practice.

Box 5.2 (from previous page; continued over)

STAKEHOLDER ENGAGEMENT ON STRATEGY

Universal rights as expressed by the UN provide both standards and the flexibility for companies to reach those standards in individual ways, something that is essential for a multinational corporation such as Novo. Fundamental human rights, such as freedom of association, freedom from discrimination and the right to health, are rights that cross cultures, but will be implemented differently depending on the nation's specific cultural heritage and national ideology. Finally, Novo's adoption of human rights ideals offers a comprehensive framework for resolving future issues. As the Senior Advisor for Ethics and Social Affairs at Novo put it, 'While many companies are adopting the labour standards this does not prepare them to deal with increasingly important societal issues like the right to health. This will become more important for many companies, particularly those involved in health sciences such as pharmaceuticals, as we saw [in the] spring [of 2001] with pharmaceutical companies in Africa.'

After adopting the Human Rights Framework in 1997, Novo established a stakeholder relationship department to develop a continual improvement system for dealing with human rights issues. Initially, the department used human rights standards as a compass to guide corporate actions. With 30 different rights explicated in the UN Declaration, the department assessed in consultation with internal stakeholders (top and middle management and employees at all levels) which values were important to the company, how to set priorities among the values, and determined first steps for implementation. This research was conducted using the same SWOT analysis techniques as used for the initial adoption of human rights, and took several field trips and two years to complete. This second round of engagement with core stakeholders asked for their input in setting strategic goals collaboratively. As Novo discovered, stakeholder engagement in setting strategic goals around human rights is best handled as an iterative process focused on learning and improvement, not a 'once and done' thing.

Box 5.2 (from previous page; continued opposite)

MOVING TO INTEGRATION

After the stakeholder relations department's stakeholder engagement processes set priorities, the company moved towards developing a strategy to raise awareness about all of the relevant human rights issues throughout the company. The priorities established a target order for implementation. For example, one of the first programmes was an equal opportunity initiative in the two major subsidiaries, Nordisk and Novozymes, for all operations. Previously, the Novo family of companies had the same governance structure. When the company de-merged its businesses into the current decentralised structure, it maintained a commitment to the human rights platform. During this process the Novo group established a charter that binds all companies to contribute to sustainable development by taking the triple-bottom-line approach. The next steps for the companies were reviewing the implications of the right to privacy and core labour rights in supply chains and customer relations. With regard to the latter, core labour rights in customer relations, Novo uses the Human Rights Framework to analyse contentious issues such as whether Novo should sell its products to governments with dictatorships that deny their citizens fundamental rights.*

CHALLENGES

Integration into strategy and operations takes time. Constant demands are placed on managers to consider economic issues, never mind community and environmental ones. Most managers are extremely busy already and, until they have fully understood the strategic importance of integrating social and ecological responsibilities alongside their economic responsibilities, incorporating these new issues can seem like 'add-ons' that take time away from business.

Universalism versus cultural relativism. Novo has found that some countries are more receptive to the Human Rights Framework than others. For example, the US has a strong bill of rights and constitution,

---

* Novo's human rights policy can be found at www.novonordisk.com/sustainability/values_in_action/human_rights.asp, accessed December 2006.

Box 5.2 (from previous page; continued opposite)

which provide the guiding legislative framework, rather than international agreements. Surprisingly, some non-Western countries such as South Africa have a higher awareness of human rights ideas than do some of the more industrialised nations.

RESULTS AND LESSONS LEARNED

Cohesiveness of initiatives. In addition to providing a tool for action planning, the Human Rights Framework brought cohesiveness to the various company initiatives. For example, since the right to a safe work environment is a fundamental principle, health and safety were brought into the responsibility management framework. While health and safety had been on Novo's agenda for 15–20 years, it had remained a function outside human resources where all the social initiatives were reported; that is, they had not been well integrated in the past.

Comprehensiveness and pre-existing resources. Since the Human Rights Framework has both breadth and depth in its declaration, it provides significant guidance to Novo on major issues relating to labour, community and the environment both today and for the future. Furthermore, the Framework is built on internationally recognised norms with the added benefit that the UN has already made investments in documents that interpret these principles.

Top-management commitment. In order to create a systemic 'responsibility' vision for a company, such as the observance of a human rights platform, Novo found it critical to establish commitment from top management. Top-management endorsement is a key to building commitment and goodwill from the managers and employees responsible for implementing the ideals embedded in the framework.

Investment in people. Novo found it needed to allocate adequate resources to implement its social and environmental commitments. The most important commitment was, of course, people's time, particularly since the focus of Novo's initiatives regarding environment, health and safety requires more behavioural change than simply investing in technology.

Box 5.2 (from previous page)

- In terms of impact on the environment?
- In our marketing and promotional efforts?
- In the way our customers perceive us?
- In our reputation?
- In our relationships with governments where we operate?
- In terms of impact on the communities in which we operate?
- Others?

● What *criticisms* might human rights, labour, environmental or other activists legitimately level against us?

● Do we expect that our suppliers will adhere to the same *standards* that we have established in our own operations? If not, what do we need to do to close this gap? Is there consistency in our standards across all of our operations? Where are the 'problem children' and what specific problems are in evidence?

● What functional areas raise *issues* that might conflict with our stated values? What are the specific concerns that an outsider might raise that we have typically overlooked?

● Would we be proud to show all of our—and our suppliers'—working environments, environmental practices, product specifications, community and environmental impacts, and government relationships to a reporter? If not, where are the problem areas? What would we like to see changed so that we could be proud to be transparent?

● What are the primary *processes* that lead to the results we want to change?
- Purchasing/sourcing?
- Personnel and human resource management, including recruitment, payment and review systems, training?
- Manufacturing? Operations? Service delivery?
- Quality systems?
- Environmental management?

- – Product development?
- – Marketing and sales practices?
- – Auditing and accounting procedures?
- – Financial analysis and reporting?
- – Government relations?
- – Others?

● How do we change these systems, who has to be involved in such change, and how will this impact on secondary and tertiary systems?

As we shall discuss in Chapter 8, implementing TRM represents a process of systemic organisational change, indeed organisational transformation, much as occurred when quality management systems were fully implemented and quality became a business imperative in the 1980s. The need for transformation towards responsibility management is clear from all of the pressures that modern companies are facing from the external environment, as well as from internal stakeholders. Competitive conditions alone make developing responsibility management a business imperative so that the company can get the most out of its stakeholder relationships and be as productive as possible. When combined with the criticisms that many companies have faced in recent times, it is clear that managing responsibility is *the* new business imperative, the one that companies hoping to gain sustainable competitive advantage in the 2000s will need to meet just to be in the game.

That is not to say that setting responsibility goals—or achieving them—is easy. But, as the lessons of the quality movement indicate, these types of systemic change are feasible and, in the end, necessary to achieve the revolutionary shifts that will be demanded of companies in the future. The NUMMI case (Box 5.3) suggests how dramatically systemic approaches such as TRM change a company's operating style as well as its stakeholder relationships.

INTEGRATION INTO MANAGEMENT SYSTEMS
MOVING FROM TROUBLE TO TRUST:
THE NUMMI CASE

It's hard to say what's the role of the union, what's the role of the company. It doesn't work that way. It's a partnership. It's a total rethinking of your role (NUMMI union leader).

A hostile union environment is not such a rare thing in the automobile industry. Yet the New United Motor Manufacturing, Inc. (NUMMI) operates in an environment characterised by peaceful labour relations based on labour–management dialogue. This case examines the new management system instituted in the NUMMI plant that supported this new paradigm of union–management collaboration.

COMPANY HISTORY AND BACKGROUND

In 1963, General Motors (GM) opened an automobile assembly plant in Fremont, California. By 1978, this plant employed over 7,200 workers. By 1982, it was closed and General Motors had a lot of sound reasons for closing the plant. GM-Fremont ranked at the bottom of GM's plants in productivity and was producing one of the worst-quality automobiles in the entire GM system. The union averaged 5,000–7,000 grievances per three-year labour contract. The plant was characterised by high use of sick leave, slowdowns, wildcat strikes and sabotage. First-line managers were carrying weapons for personal protection and daily absenteeism was almost 20%. Drug abuse and alcoholism plagued the workforce.

There was a climate of fear and mistrust between management and the workers. George Nano, union representative at this GM plant, described labour relations there: 'It was war. At GM we had to fight for everything. Management just did not seem to care. And when management doesn't care, workers won't care either.'

Box 5.3 (continued over)

Sources: Adler and Cole 1993; O'Reilly and Pfeffer 2000

In 1983 General Motors signed a letter of intent with Toyota to re-open the plant, now named the New United Motor Manufacturing, Inc. (NUMMI). Toyota wanted to gain a foothold in the US market, learn about working with US suppliers, and see if its manufacturing and management approaches could work with US workers. GM needed a small car (the Nova) to add to its product line and hoped to learn about Toyota's production system. Doug Fraser, then president of the United Auto Workers (UAW) union, saw this as an interesting opportunity and committed the union to work with the new venture. Don Ephlin, UAW head for GM also made the commitment. The commitment of top leadership from both union and management is one of the necessary components of TRM.

NEW RELATIONSHIPS

How was the plant able to shed its history of antagonistic union–management relations and develop new relationships from the institutional to interpersonal level? The explanation is simple: the difference in management systems and approaches. New management, which mainly consisted of Toyota managers, introduced the Toyota system of lean manufacturing, which depends crucially on trust and respect for workers. This system emphasises teamwork, job security, employee involvement and worker self-confidence. The system makes all employees responsible for quality and safety and provides a Jidoka* method (the *andon* cord) for any person to stop the line to get help with a quality or safety problem. This manufacturing process creates empowerment through job design allowing employees to make decisions about improvement, a core feature of TRM's innovation element. Even though the estimated cost

---

* Jidoka is one of NUMMI's basic concepts; it holds that quality should be ensured in the production process itself. This means not allowing defective parts to go from one workstation to the next. Jidoka refers to machines or the production line itself being able to stop automatically in abnormal conditions (for example, when a machine breaks down or when defective parts are produced). Jidoka is also used when team members encounter a problem at their workstation. They are responsible for correcting the problem; if they cannot, they can stop the line. The objective of Jidoka can be summed up as: ensuring quality 100% of the time; preventing equipment breakdowns; and using manpower efficiently (www.nummi.com).

Box 5.3 (from previous page; continued opposite)

of line downtime is US$15,000 per minute, the cord is routinely pulled over 100 times per day (O'Reilly and Pfeffer 2000).

This new system also promotes an egalitarian culture and team approach. Now NUMMI has three levels of management, compared with five or six levels at other GM plants. All workers at NUMMI are part of 3–6 people multifunctional teams, run by a team leader, who is not a part of management, but a union member selected jointly by management and the union.

O'Reilly and Pfeffer (2002) document: 'From the beginning, the NUMMI system has relied on a unique relationship between the union and management . . . [union] has supported the NUMMI production system, including the team concept, . . . job classifications, non-confrontational problem solving (asking "why", not "who")' (O'Reilly and Pfeffer 2002). In return for this support, NUMMI management recognised from day one the same union (UAW, Local 2244) that represented workers at GM-Fremont. As part of this negotiation they agreed to pay union-scale wages and reappoint the union bargaining committee. These management agreements reflect the incorporation of international standards into GM's foundational values, an important component of TRM's inspiration element. In a similar trust-building move, the management asked union leaders under the old system to resume their role and agreed that team leaders (the key production position at NUMMI) should be selected jointly by union and management. Finally, management committed to a no lay-off policy* and signed a new collective bargaining agreement.

The new collective agreement starts by stating (NUMMI internal document 1983, cited in O'Reilly and Pfeffer 2002): 'Both parties are undertaking this new proposed relationship with the full intention of fostering an innovative labour relations structure, minimising traditional adversarial roles and emphasising mutual trust and good faith.'

This contract served as a platform for identifying and communicating a shared union–management vision, a crucial aspect

---

* This was an important move; 80% of NUMMI workers feel that job security is the most important aspect of working at NUMMI (O'Reilly and Pfeffer 2000: 189).

Box 5.3 (from previous page; continued over)

of TRM. Furthermore, this contract allowed the union, the premier internal stakeholder group, to participate in defining the terms of engagement with the company, yet another cornerstone of TRM. The union–management vision of trust and mutual respect is clearly evident when comparing the new and old contracts (O'Reilly and Pfeffer 2000; see Table 5.2).

Interestingly enough, the old contract ran to over 1,400 pages in eight booklets, while the new contract needed only one booklet of less than 100 pages. Why use paper when the trust is already established? As one of the NUMMI union leaders put it (*San Jose Mercury News* 1990, cited in O'Reilly and Pfeffer 2002): 'It's hard to say what's the role of the union, what's the role of the company. It doesn't work that way. It's a partnership. It's a total rethinking of your role.'

OUTCOMES

Now NUMMI is one of the best plants in the industry. The plant employs over 4,000 union members and produces an average of 87 vehicles per employee, far above the 50 cars per worker that both Saturn and Buick City average, the most efficient GM facilities (O'Reilly and Pfeffer 2002). In 1998 NUMMI won the National Association of Manufacturers' award for excellence. The award noted that this plant managed a changeover to a new model in the remarkable time of only five days and took only 30 days to reach full production. The quality of the new vehicles, already one of the highest rated, was nearly 50% better than the old version, while the cost-reduction targets through the launch were exceeded by 86%. In addition the workforce made over 3.2 suggestions per person in 1998, of which 81% were adopted. Over 86% of the plant's team members made suggestions that year that led to the savings of over US$27 million (Cushman and King 1997).

RESULTS AND LESSONS LEARNED

Inspiration
Senior leadership commitment by both the management and the union is necessary to create organisation-wide support for the culture

Box 5.3 (from previous page; continued opposite)

change necessary in the new union–management partnership and commitment to a common vision.

Recognition of international standards, such as freedom of association, provide a fundamental commitment by the company to a baseline set of values that help build trust with employees.

Vision identification and communication. NUMMI's guiding principles are the foundation of their production system. These include recognising human worth and dignity, developing individual performance, developing team performance and improving the work environment. The spirit of these ideals is reflected in the text of the contract.

Safety and learning features are built into the manufacturing process, as seen in the Jidoka method. This process also builds trust between workers and management by setting priorities for safety over profits.

Improvement and innovation
Job design promotes empowerment of front-line employees, including responsibility to make decisions regarding problems in production.

Stakeholder engagement
Allowing stakeholders to define their terms of engagement with the company, as seen in the joint union–management-appointed team managers.

Box 5.3 (from previous page)

OLD GM CONTRACT	NEW NUMMI CONTRACT
UAW and GM 'recognize their respective responsibilities under federal, state, and local laws relating to fair employment practices'.	UAW and NUMMI 'will exhibit mutual trust, understanding, and sincerity, and, to the fullest extent possible, will avoid confrontational tactics'.
'Employees will be laid off and rehired in accordance with local seniority agreements', with management giving 24 hour notice.	'The company will take affirmative measures before laying off any employees, including such measures as the reduction of salaries of its officers and management.'

TABLE 5.2 NUMMI: old and new contracts

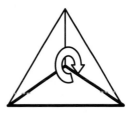

6

Improvement and innovation systems

Responsibility management is fundamentally aimed at fostering continual *innovation and improvement* in management systems that affect stakeholders and the natural environment. Leaders can accomplish the objective of continual improvement in TRM approaches by carefully designing improvement right into the system and recognising that, in many ways, the company always needs to strive for improvement in its stakeholder relationships and the impacts or outcomes of its activities. By using the *indicators* that will be discussed in the next chapter and creating a continual improvement system similar to that used for continual quality improvement, companies focus on improving what is being done today for better results tomorrow.

6.1 Improvement and innovation

Responsibility management approaches use iterative processes focused on making all of the company's stakeholder relationships and impacts better over time. The innovation and improvement components of TRM involve establishing processes for remediation of wrongs, improvement where needed, innovation of new ideas, processes and practices, and ongoing organisational learning. Data from measurement and accountability systems, discussed in the next chapter as 'Indicators', provide managers with the feedback necessary to create innovations and improvements in their systems and management practices.

A key step in developing innovation and improvement systems is to provide guidance and structures that encourage responsible practices. The goal is to provide an emphasis on continued organisational learning and development towards ever-more responsible practice. Four major processes can be helpful in thinking through the innovation and improvement systems: remediation, continual improvement, creating a learning organisation, and focusing on results.

6.2 Remediation

Remediation involves fixing what is wrong. Obviously, the first step towards managing responsibility is to identify problem areas, as the gap and diagnostic analysis detailed in the previous chapter suggests. But identifying the problems is not the end of the process; it is only the beginning. More important is figuring out how to resolve the identified problems, address concerns raised by stakeholders through the stakeholder dialogue process, or reduce gaps between espoused values and goals and realised ones. This is the remediation process.

Remediation links to the foundational values agreed by the international community and the specific responsibility vision of the corporation. Remediation also addresses specific problems by immediately eliminating practices that are intolerable under the foundational values and working towards resolving problems that stakeholders find unacceptable.

IMPROVEMENT AND INNOVATION
H&M: BUILDING SUPPLIER RELATIONS THROUGH KNOWLEDGE SHARING

As retail firms continue to outsource production and simultaneously face consumer pressure to act socially and environmentally responsibly, supply chain management requires consideration of cost and quality, as well as labour and environmental management. Clothing manufacturing entails numerous production processes, often including various chemicals. This case details how H&M, a clothing and cosmetics retailer, has expanded internal job responsibilities to track and share emerging research on chemical restrictions with suppliers that support its environmental mission.

COMPANY HISTORY AND BACKGROUND

Established in 1947, H&M (Hennes & Mauritz) sell clothing and cosmetics in around 1,200 stores in 22 countries. Internet sales are offered in Sweden, Denmark and Finland and throughout Scandinavia by mail order. Their business concept is 'Fashion and quality at the best price', resulting in sales of about 400 million articles a year. H&M sells women's, men's and children's clothes (half of which are made in Europe, the rest mostly in Asia) from about 700 suppliers. The company employs approximately 50,000 employees (www.hm.com/us, accessed December 2006).

ENVIRONMENTAL POLICY MOVING DOWN THE SUPPLY CHAIN

The first statement in H&M's environmental policy incorporates a fundamental principle of TRM: feedback systems that promote transparency, accountability and learning. 'Continuous improvements are significant for all H&M activities. This includes our environmental effort, which is conducted within the framework of our business operations' (www.hm.com/us/corporateresponsibility/ environment_ _environment.nhtml, accessed December 2006). This commitment to periodic review and assessments, a tenet of TRM's vision–setting process, is also evident in H&M's Environmental Policy,

Box 6.1 (continued over)

which is now in its third version. Ingrid Schullstrom, Head of Quality Control, described the current policy revision as a 'more down–up approach, focusing first on concrete issues at the bottom and then translating this up into policy'. She attributes this approach to the fact that H&M is a retailer rather than a manufacturing facility. During the latest policy review the top management endorsed the newest version in 1999, reflecting another critical TRM element: top-management commitment.

The H&M environmental policy discusses traditional issues such as health and safety, legal requirements and building requirements. In addition, the policy has three unique components relating to learning, improvement and supplier relations, an increasingly important nexus of corporate accountability. The first of these requires H&M to update the business and suppliers on environmental news and legislation, referred to as shared learning in the TRM model. The second is a pledge to develop new and continuously improve existing environmental requirements concerning the purchase of products and services. The third area is co-operation of suppliers, achieved by having all merchandise suppliers agree to abide by established chemical restrictions. This commitment combines TRM's vision and stakeholder engagement elements by having the suppliers formally commit to supporting the environmental principles. These supplier commitments are an essential part of H&M's commitment detailed in its environmental policy for contributing 'to the reduction of environmental harm during the production of our merchandise' since it outsources all production.

H&M's chemical restrictions are based on the strictest country standards in which retail stores are located. It has updated its restrictions six times since 2995, most recently in 2005. These restrictions concern chemicals used in the production of clothing as well as other products sold by H&M. With the precautionary principle in environmental policy, the company tries to keep abreast of the latest developments through watching the positions of environmental thought leaders, such as Greenpeace, regarding various chemicals. Typically, when the scientific community identifies chemicals they consider obsolete, H&M starts to test products to see if these

Box 6.1 (from previous page; continued opposite)

chemicals are contained in any of their products. H&M goes beyond mandating restrictions to suppliers; rather, it tries to find alternatives to banned substances and shares these ideas with its suppliers and assists them in phasing out old products.

Two critical employees in these efforts are the chemist and the environmental co-ordinator, both members of the environmental team. The chemist follows the recent scientific literature and co-ordinates the testing in production offices. The suppliers are provided with a list of banned chemicals and must sign a commitment that they will abide by this agreement when sourcing H&M product lines. In the document of banned chemicals H&M includes alternatives for the prohibited materials. The company offers further help and consultation to the suppliers if requested. This monitoring of emerging standards occurs through the expanded view of job design, simply including these responsibilities in the chemist's job scope. The environmental co-ordinator works closely with the chemist making sure that all the specialists in the production offices are trained to advise staff in these facilities on environmental compliance issues such as prohibited chemicals.

Besides educating the suppliers, the company makes an effort to inform its own employees about environmental matters. For example, H&M's environmental policies and chemical restrictions are published on its intranet, providing information on sourcing and purchasing to employees throughout the organisation. Thus, as standards are changed H&M can inform employees through the intranet. The TRM idea of training is evident in the H&M commitment to educating suppliers on these hazards in its efforts to inform both suppliers and employees.

RESTRICTIONS TO KNOWLEDGE TRANSFER: PVC EXAMPLE

H&M's PVC (polyvinyl chloride) reduction effort is an example of its continuous commitment to improvement stated in its environmental policy. PVC chemicals have been linked to cancer and kidney damage and possible interference with the reproductive system and in human development. Since 1997, the company has been phasing out PVC plastics with the goal of total elimination in 2002. The first step in the

Box 6.1 (from previous page; continued over)

initiative began with identifying PVC in all products, then offering replacement ideas appropriate to a given product or supplier. Schullstrom reported that replacing this chemical alone is projected to take five years. One of the initial challenges was that suppliers reported the absence of alternatives. This led to finding best-practice alternatives for certain suppliers and sharing ideas with suppliers in different countries. A large part of the information sharing was simply technology transfer by telling suppliers that in other countries reliable alternatives could be sourced. Sharing knowledge and learning gained from enacting goals and sharing with both external and internal groups, as in this case, is a fundamental part of innovation in TRM. For more details, see H&M's 2005 CSR report (www.hm.com/us/corporateresponsibility/csrreporting__csrreporting.nhtml, accessed December 2006).

RESULTS AND LESSONS LEARNED

Production changes require several stages. Phasing out chemicals requires several steps: (1) identifying problem chemicals, (2) testing for its presence in your products, (3) researching alternatives, and (4) sharing technology with suppliers.

Clear vision statements help provide a clear framework for action such as the H&M Environmental Policy statement on continuous improvement. These statements can also provide clear direction for a company's terms of business with suppliers.

Supplier compliance requires building internal and external human resource capacity. Supplier compliance was accomplished through the internal job design, such as allocating specific responsibilities to the staff chemist and environmental co-ordinator. Likewise, supplier capacity was increased through providing training at production facilities on environmental issues.

Improvement and innovation requires knowledge sharing. Through updating the prohibited chemicals list and offering best-practice alternatives, H&M acted as a conduit for conveying critical information to suppliers from both the scientific and the business communities.

Box 6.1 (from previous page)

6.3 Continual improvement

Improvement and innovation means taking processes or systems that may or may not be working reasonably well now and making them better. It means generating new ideas, new products, new systems and new approaches to organising. While no human system will ever be perfect, the attention to quality management in some companies today suggests that continual improvement is indeed both a desirable and an achievable goal. Improving a company's systems and stakeholder relationships can add significantly to the bottom line, as fewer resources will be wasted, more satisfied employees are likely to be more productive, and creating the necessary internal systems and infrastructure will be easier. Employees are the most critical resource that a company has for improving its responsibility management systems because they do the work of the organisation day to day.

6.3.1 The employee link

Employee loyalty, commitment and productive energy *do* matter to the success and health of the firm, as a considerable amount of research suggests (Huselid 1995; Huselid *et al.* 1997; O'Reilly and Pfeffer 2000; Pfeffer 1998; Pfeffer and Veiga 1999). For example, treating employees well is essential for generating high levels of productivity over a long period of time. Treating employees well generates commitment to the organisation's vision, particularly if that vision is shared with employees and they understand what their role is in accomplishing it. Treating employees well also generates a willingness to contribute to achieving the organisation's goals by improving problem areas, reducing wastefulness and generating innovations that can improve productivity.

Despite the fact that we know how valuable employees are, many companies still operate on failed assumptions (Pfeffer and Veiga 1999). Their employee (and other stakeholder) practices, that is, differ greatly from their rhetoric and some even mistreat employees. Still, highly successful firms know what to do to treat employees well and, in many cases, they also extend those operating principles and practices to other stakeholders through their stakeholder engagement systems. These successful companies engage in a number of employee-specific practices that provide employees with the sense of meaning and contribution that are important to long-term productivity. Some of these practices are directly counter to current management practices which result in erosion of employee loyalty (and correspondingly community health as well) and capacity. Table 6.1 highlights some of the actual practices that researchers Jeffrey Pfeffer and John Veiga have found in use in highly effective companies.

Employees, like other stakeholders, need and want to feel that they can make a contribution to improving their own working situation, their own productivity and their own lives. Companies that recognise this reality can tap into a major resource for innovation and improvement, an essential aspect of responsibility management.

6.3.2 Other stakeholders

Quality programmes, following the advice of management guru Dr W. Edwards Deming, typically focus on continual quality improvement through emphasis on statistical process controls and quality management. TRM approaches ensure that customer, community, supplier, owner, employee, activist and other stakeholder relationships are on solid ground and that trust is being built. A study of quality programmes suggests the characteristics that can be found in world-class companies in both production and service industries. These characteristics of world-class plants and organisations, we suggest, are the same as those that need to be embedded in the improvement processes of responsibility management to enable companies to develop excellent stakeholder relationships (Poirier and Houser 1993). Table 6.2 illustrates what scholars Charles C. Poirier and William F. Houser find to be the key characteristics of 'world-class' companies.

Employment security	Provides job security even when productivity improves. Retains knowledgeable, productive workers, builds commitment and retention, decreases costs associated with lay-offs (including training and recruitment)
Selective hiring	Creates 'cult-like' cultures built on common values. Requires large applicant pool, clarity about critical skills and attributes needed, clear sense of job requirements, and screening on attributes difficult to change through training
Self-managed teams and decentralisation	Teams substitute peer-based control for hierarchical control Increases shared responsibility for outcomes, stimulating initiative and effort. Removes levels of management (cost). Ideas are shared and creative solutions found
Comparatively high compensation contingent on organisation performance	High pay produces organisational success. Retains expertise and experience, rewards and reinforces high performance Rewards the whole as well as individual effort. Requires employee training to understand links between ownership and rewards
Extensive training	Values knowledge and skills (generalist, not specialist). Relies on front-line employee skill and initiative for problem-solving and innovation, responsibility for quality. Can be source of competitive advantage

TABLE 6.1 Employee practices of successful organisations
(continued over)

Source: Summarised from Pfeffer and Veiga 1999

Reduction of status differences	Premised on belief that high performance is achieved when ideas, skills, efforts of all are fully tapped. To do this requires reducing differences among levels, symbolically (language and labels, physical space, dress), and substantively (reduction of wage inequality across levels)
Sharing information	To create a high-trust organisation requires shared information across levels on issues such as financial performance, strategy and organisational measures. Helps everyone know where contributions come from, where they stand

TABLE 6.1 (from previous page)

WORLD–CLASS PLANT	**WORLD–CLASS SERVICE ORGANISATION**
● Safety ● Involved and committed workforce ● Just-in-time manufacturing and deliveries to customers ● Focus on product flow ● Preventative/predictive maintenance ● Bottlenecks managed ● Total quality management programme ● Fast set-ups ● Extremely low inventories ● Supportive policies/procedures	● Accessibility and follow-up by employees ● Competence (required skills and knowledge, proactive) ● Attitude (positive, flexible, continuous improvement) ● Communication ● Credibility ● Features/innovation in services ● Responsiveness ● Tangible results

TABLE 6.2 Characteristics of world–class quality, and TRM, operations

Source: Poirier and Houser 1993

6.4 Create a learning organisation

A key component of responsibility management systems is that they establish an environment within the company for ongoing learning: that is, companies using TRM approaches become learning organisations.[1] They do this through a process of continual organisational change and development that devolves responsibility for responsibility management throughout the organisation. In many respects there are similar criteria on which performance excellence can be assessed between TRM and the quality movement, as Table 6.3, which compares the Baldrige Quality Award criteria with the criteria for performance excellence in TRM, indicates. This table provides a synopsis of some of the key elements needed to create a learning—or continually improving—organisation around responsibility management.

The quality movement also articulated a set of important principles, known as Deming's 14 points, by which organisations could begin to move their practices towards higher levels of quality as well as continual improvement. In Table 6.4 there is a similar roadmap for companies to follow when they are implementing TRM.

As can readily be seen in the adaptation of quality principles to TRM, the expansion of the set of stakeholders for whom responsibility management matters means that an even broader and more systemic focus is needed to implement responsibility management than is necessary for quality management. Yet what is also clear is that management knows both what to do and how to go about making the necessary changes, because the underlying organisational transformation processes are well known through past experience with quality management systems.

6.4.1 Make a shift of mind

Taking the necessary actions to create a learning organisation means understanding the need for the organisational transformation in the first

---

1 Peter Senge (1990) wrote the seminal work on learning organisations in *The Fifth Discipline: The Art and Practice of the Learning Organization* (updated edition 2006).

BALDRIGE NATIONAL QUALITY AWARD CRITERIA FOR PERFORMANCE EXCELLENCE	TRM CRITERIA FOR PERFORMANCE EXCELLENCE
1. Continuous quality improvement	1. Continual responsibility improvement process ensures that TRM standards are met
2. Meeting customers' requirements	2. Lives up to expectations of global business, NGO and governmental communities regarding responsible relationships with employees, suppliers, customers and communities through sustainable management practices
3. Long-range planning	3. Long-range planning
4. Increased employee involvement	4. Meeting employees' expectations about responsible practices through engagement and dialogue
5. Process management	5. Increased stakeholder engagement and management of stakeholder relationships, practices and impacts through attention to systems, processes and outcomes
6. Competitive benchmarking	6. Competitive benchmarking of responsibility systems, including systems/process management for continual responsibility improvement

TABLE 6.3 Baldrige criteria extended to total responsibility management (continued opposite)

Source: www.quality.nist.gov/Business_Criteria.htm

BALDRIGE NATIONAL QUALITY AWARD CRITERIA FOR PERFORMANCE EXCELLENCE	TRM CRITERIA FOR PERFORMANCE EXCELLENCE
7. Team-based problem-solving	7. Employee, supplier and customer involvement in meeting standards and problem-solving
8. Constant measurement of results	8. Constant assessment of results, externally verified auditing process, communication and reporting out to stakeholders
9. Closer relationships with customers	9. Closer, engaged and mutually respectful stakeholder relationships
10. Management commitment	10. Top-management commitment, management commitment at all levels, employee and supplier commitment. Clear articulation of vision, core values and strategies for continual improvement of stakeholder relations and performance assessment

TABLE 6.3 (from previous page)

DEMING'S ORIGINAL 14 POINTS	ADAPTATION TO TRM
1. Create and publish to all employees a statement of the aims and purposes of the company or other organisation. The management must demonstrate constantly their commitment to this statement	1. Create and publish to employees and other key stakeholders a statement that includes the vision, core values, purposes, and stakeholders to whom the organisation is accountable. Management must consistently demonstrate commitment to the statement
2. Learn the new philosophy, top management and everybody	2. Vision, values and purposes of the enterprise must be clear to every stakeholder involved with the company, particularly employees who are responsible for implementation
3. Understand the purpose of inspection of processes and reduction of cost	3. Understand the need for both transparency of and accountability for corporate practices in assuring that they meet globally accepted standards of responsibility
4. End the practice of awarding business on the basis of price tag alone	4. End wage and price arbitrage (the 'race to the bottom' in wages) and focus on working with employees and suppliers who provide good-quality products and services at reasonable prices in accordance with all standards and global norms

TABLE 6.4 Deming's 14 points extended to TRM (continued opposite)

Source: Deming 1986

DEMING'S ORIGINAL 14 POINTS	ADAPTATION TO TRM
5. Improve constantly and forever the system of production and service	5. Improve constantly and forever responsible practices with respect to all stakeholders, particularly employees and the natural environment
6. Institute training	6. Build understanding and commitment through training, communication and stakeholder engagement
7. Teach and institute leadership	7. Teach and institute leadership at all levels within the organisation and in interactions with stakeholders
8. Drive out fear. Create trust. Create a climate for innovation	8. Drive out fear and create trusting relationships with stakeholders. Create a climate of engagement, dialogue and innovation about the responsibility inherent in corporate systems and practices
9. Optimise towards the aims and purposes of the company the efforts of teams, groups and staff areas	9. Optimise towards responsible practice and the mutuality of interests of important stakeholder groups
10. Eliminate exhortations for the workforce	10. Eliminate irresponsible practices within systems, with respect to the workforce, other stakeholders and the natural environment

TABLE 6.4 (from previous page; continued over)

DEMING'S ORIGINAL 14 POINTS	ADAPTATION TO TRM
11. (a) Eliminate numerical quotas for production. Instead, learn and institute methods for improvement. (b) Eliminate MBO (management by objective). Instead, learn the capabilities of processes and how to improve them	11. (a) Institute a responsible vision with baseline foundational values and methods of continual improvement. (b) Learn methods for continually improving relationships with stakeholders and corporate practices
12. Remove barriers that rob people of pride in workmanship	12. Remove barriers that rob employees and other stakeholders of the ability to accept responsibility for impacts
13. Encourage education and self-improvement for everyone	13. Encourage education and continual improvement of relationships, responsibilities and results for key stakeholders
14. Take action to accomplish the transformation	14. Take action to accomplish the transformation

TABLE 6.4 (from previous page)

place. This may well encompass a significant change in mind-set, or what the author of *The Fifth Discipline*, Peter Senge,[2] calls *metanoia*—a shift of mind. This shift of mind involves, first, accepting responsibility for managing responsibility and accepting the reality that stakeholder relationships do matter in today's world. The next step in the shift of mind is to begin taking action—to actually implement the steps necessary to manage for responsibility, as noted above.

2   These steps are derived from Senge 1990 (rev. edn 2006).

6.4.2 Understand the patterns

Systemic or systems thinking is also a necessary element of creating a learning organisation. Many patterns exist in organisations that are damaging to productivity or to stakeholder relationships. Understanding these patterns, which Senge calls archetypes, can help to avoid the negative consequences that result when responsibility management is either ignored or goes awry.

6.4.3 Find leverage points for change

Equally important to creating system change is finding where to begin. Senge calls these potential points of change leverage points. In TRM, leverage points can potentially be found in some of the following areas:

- Areas of employee or worker dissatisfaction

- Arenas where employees can be empowered to take personal responsibility for their own working conditions, the relationships with suppliers and customers, or their own work

- Reward systems

- Feedback and stakeholder engagement systems, which can provide critical information needed to understand where the problems are in the first place. Note that feedback needs to include employees, as well as external groups critical of the company's practices for it to be realistic and worthwhile.

- Supplier relationships and sourcing processes

Creating a learning organisation involves five specific skill sets, according to Peter Senge. As we think about what is needed to create learning for continual responsibility management improvement, the essence of TRM, we can extend these five skill sets to TRM. Box 6.2 adapts Senge's 'disciplines' for creating learning organisations to TRM to illustrate what skills and competences are needed in the transformation—and ongoing improvement and innovation—processes.

BUILDING LEARNING ORGANISATIONS FOR TOTAL RESPONSIBILITY MANAGEMENT

The following five skills are the essence of creating a learning organisation, as identified by Senge in *The Fifth Discipline*. Here they are adapted to TRM.

1. **Personal mastery**. Personal mastery is the discipline of personal growth and learning, which creates an ability for individuals to continually expand their ability to learn and create the 'results they truly seek' in life. Applied to TRM, personal mastery means that individuals can understand their own role and contribution in the perspective of the common good created by the vision and values of the enterprise as a whole. Personal mastery also means that individual employees and other stakeholders take responsibility to ensure that what they do has the most positive impacts on other stakeholders that is feasible. Further, individuals with personal mastery work hard to think through the consequences of their own performance and decisions, or what Senge terms seeing reality clearly.

2. **Mental models**. Understanding mental models means realising that everyone comes to a situation with a set of ideas in place, or what management scholar Chris Argyris (1993) calls 'theories in use'. Applied to TRM, that may mean that individuals approach managing for responsibility and other improvements with ideas such as 'That's not what we do here' or 'You can't measure that'. Similar mental models informed the quality movement and, as we all know, were eventually changed to recognise that quality management, like responsibility management, improves company performance. According to Senge, the discipline of mental models involves surfacing, testing and ultimately improving internal pictures or images of how the organisation does and should work. By doing this explicitly in TRM, stakeholders can bring their unique perspectives into the organisation, share them and resolve differences where they will inevitably occur. Even if differences

Box 6.2 (continued opposite)

are irreconcilable, knowing what they are will enable better decisions to be made.

3. **Shared vision**. Shared vision means that every stakeholder of an enterprise knows 'what we want to create' together. Of course, shared vision in a TRM context means that the organisation's responsibility vision, underlying values, and explicit strategies and practices by which the vision is to be achieved are widely shared and recognised. Because most people want to contribute to the success of their organisation when its values are constructive (Waddock 2002), creating a vision about managing responsibility that is widely shared in the organisation is an essential element of TRM.

4. **Team learning**. Developing effective and highly performing teams is critical to developing a learning organisation. This task can be accomplished only when everyone is empowered to do his or her best and knows what direction makes sense for the organisation. In a TRM context not only are employees empowered to do their jobs well and, in Peter Drucker's (1970) sense, effectively (i.e. doing the right thing as well as being efficient), but they are also involved in the continual loop of feedback, re-energising effort and learning that provides for ongoing improvement. That is, they know what the explicit responsibility and organisational goals are and work hard to develop teams that can accomplish those goals effectively through shared power, information and resources that create a level playing field for all.

5. **Understanding system dynamics**. Systems thinking is what Senge calls the 'fifth discipline', the underpinning of creating a learning organisation. As Senge points out, understanding the organisation as a system makes patterns clearer and helps change agents figure out how to develop quickly and effectively. This means figuring out where the leverage points for change are and how to apply those levers effectively. In TRM, important levers are:

Box 6.2 (from previous page; continued over)

- *The reward system.* You get the behaviour you reward, so identification of responsibility goals that can be rewarded in multiple ways is a key to effectiveness.

- *Feedback and improvement systems.* Measuring and reporting on the success of meeting responsibility objectives is a key to developing an appropriate reward and incentive system. How measures for assessing the triple bottom lines of economic, societal and environmental objectives can be developed will be discussed in the next chapter.

- *The organisational structure.* Strategy determines structure, according to the classical theory of strategic management (Chandler 1962). But we also know that structure determines strategy; hence reporting and responsibility relationships require careful consideration in responsibility management. If responsibility for ensuring that standards are met is diffused throughout the enterprise (as, for example, responsibility for quality is now diffused), then the appropriate structure for ensuring that responsibility objectives are met needs to be determined by those who will be involved. Shared power facilitates continual improvement, as do . . .

- *Information and communication systems.* Most stakeholders today want to know what is happening in companies about which they are concerned: that is, they are demanding both *accountability* and *transparency*, whether they are inside or outside the organisation. Thus, the importance of measuring responsibility and stakeholder impacts has never been greater, or as well understood as it is today, as the next sections will document.

- *Stakeholder dialogue.* Engaging stakeholders in dialogue helps the company to understand how its actions, impacts and practices are perceived both by those friendly to the company and by its critics. Additionally, stakeholder engagement processes can be an important source of information that feeds back into the company's improvement and learning processes, helping it better meet the needs of customers, as well as other stakeholders.

Box 6.2 (from previous page)

6.5 Focus on results

Approaches to quality management use a simple cycle to frame the assessment of the results achieved as well as the need for improvements and innovations. Called 'The Deming Cycle', this cycle uses Deming's famous 14 points for reducing variation to improve quality in a sequence of 'plan, do, study (or check) and act'. We noted earlier how readily Deming's 14 points extend to TRM. The outcomes of productive processes in a company are its results—and the consequent impacts on stakeholders and the natural environment, or on what has come to be called the triple bottom line of economic, societal and environmental impacts. The responsibility measurement systems help a company to assess its performance multi-dimensionally and with a multiple-bottom-line orientation that permits comprehensive performance assessment along traditional financial as well as stakeholder and ecological lines. Thus, companies need to figure out how to measure stakeholder impacts and the attendant responsibility. It is to this issue we turn in the next chapter.

7

Indicators

MEASURING
RESPONSIBILITY MANAGEMENT

The **improvement** and **innovation** elements of TRM create a significant demand for companies to broaden how they measure performance. To measure responsibility, new **indicators** need to be added to financial and quality management systems, in what we call 'plus indicators'. Indicators for TRM focus on stakeholders, and on the triple bottom lines of economic, societal and environment issues.

7.1 Responsibility measurement system

Measurement of the impacts and responsibility of both the processes and results of systems and corporate practices in a multiple (at least triple, i.e. economic, social and ecological)-bottom-line framework is a critical component of implementing and understanding a responsibility vision. Responsibility management measures focus on:

- The company's vision, mission and stated values

- The company's stakeholder and environmental operating practices and impacts

- The company's economic, social and environmental performance

By developing responsibility assessment systems, particularly by paying attention to comparability across companies and within the company across units, companies can increase the credibility and reliability of their reports. By making the results available to relevant stakeholders, frequently by publishing a triple-bottom-line or multiple-bottom-line report (or separate financial, environmental and social reports in some cases), companies assure that they are meeting increasingly vociferous external demands for transparency and accountability.

Measurement systems evaluate stakeholder impacts and performance through strategic and functional area assessments, as well as by assessing the extent to which the company actually lives up to its responsibility vision, mission and stated values. Data gathered through measurement procedures, information technology systems and responsibility auditing practices provide *a baseline for continually improving operating practices*, as noted in the previous chapter. Such assessments work by highlighting urgent situations, illustrating dramatically where gaps between rhetoric and practice exist or where stakeholders perceive problems, providing feedback on progress, and fostering accountability to internal and external stakeholders through valid and reliable assessment/auditing practices transparently revealed to key stakeholders.

7.2 Value–added responsibility management

Many people assume that managing more responsibly necessarily means making less money. That is, they assume there is a trade-off between responsibility and profitability. Frequently, however, the opposite is true: by behaving more responsibly companies can often actually *improve* their traditional bottom-line results, as the examples in the boxes indicate. For example, it does not cost any more to treat workers with dignity and respect, yet productivity can improve when they are well treated, as a huge amount of research on employee productivity now suggests.

EMPLOYEE RELATIONS

A leading regional insurer needed to develop a strategy for reducing its high employee turnover in dead-end positions. An intensive study of employee policies resulted in improvements in job satisfaction with the potential to raise net profits by 7%, increase worker employability and create a new revenue stream to offset replacement costs.

Box 7.1

Source: Waddock and Smith 2000

QUALITY MANAGEMENT

A *Fortune* 500 firm in the throes of downsizing helped adversely affected employees, reduced operational inefficiencies associated with making critical decisions under pressure, and avoided potential legal action and employee violence by implementing policies and procedures recommended after an intensive assessment of its operations. The assessment also resulted in a strategy for a 10% reduction in medical costs and absenteeism totalling more than US$450,000. Implementation of a quality management system was simultaneously estimated to increase productivity and effective manufacturing capacity, also reduce production cycle time, and decrease operating costs by two to three times over a three- to five-year period.

Box 7.2

Source: Waddock and Smith 2000

ENVIRONMENTAL MANAGEMENT

A leading multinational manufacturing company had won numerous environmental awards. Nonetheless, the company found after an analysis of its environmental policies that it could reduce the high costs of regulatory compliance by teaming research and development, production and sales departments to improve production efficiencies and eliminate waste at source. The strategy was estimated to save nearly US$200,000, excluding the reduction.

Box 7.3

Source: Waddock and Smith 2000

MANAGING SUPPLY CHAINS FOR RESPONSIBILITY

The following two examples are from a study of supply chains of multinational firms:

> For getting companies to realise the value of doing things the right way, top management has to be made aware that eventually it will benefit the company. Safe workplaces are more productive . . . We improved the ventilation in [a production area] and this resulted in defects falling to 2% from 7 or 8%, while productivity went up 20%.

> We improved airflows, which resulted in a 2° temperature drop. This, along with other changes, resulted in, according to our estimate, an increase in productivity of 10–15% while cutting defect rates by 75%.

Box 7.4

Source: Waddock and Bodwell 2002

7.3 The key is measurement

The key to making the link between performance and responsibility is learning how to measure responsibility performance, much the same problem that was initially faced in the quality movement when people believed 'you can't measure quality'. Many people today similarly and erroneously believe that 'you can't measure responsibility'. Yet numerous new approaches are now being devised to measure the responsibility of a company's practices, particularly as they affect stakeholders. One of the most notable approaches is that of the Global Reporting Initiative (GRI), a multi-stakeholder initiative that aims to devise and implement globally accepted responsibility and sustainability reporting guidelines that are comparable across companies operating in different industries, much as generally accepted accounting principles are standardised.

Like many of the emerging initiatives on measurement, GRI emphasises the triple bottom lines of economic, environmental and social issues. Box 7.5 provides the GRI's three elements of sustainability applied to companies:

THE GRI SUSTAINABILITY REPORTING GUIDELINES FOCUS ON THREE INTERLINKED ELEMENTS

Economic. Including, for example, wages and benefits, labour productivity, job creation, expenditures on outsourcing, expenditures on research and development, and investments in training and other forms of human capital. The economic elements include, but are not limited to, financial information.

Social. Including, for example, workplace health and safety, employee retention, labour rights, human rights, and wages and working conditions at outsourced operations.

Environmental. Including, for example, impacts of processes, products and services on air, water, land, biodiversity and human health.

Box 7.5

Source: GRI 2002

In addition to the Global Reporting Initiative, the International Organisation for Standardisation (ISO), which promulgates quality and environmental standards that are widely used in businesses, announced in 2004 that is it is developing voluntary standards for corporate responsibility by 2008. According to ISO, the standards will not be a management system standard nor for certification purposes; nonetheless, they are expected to provide guidance to companies for managing their responsibilities to stakeholders.

As may be apparent, the three legs of the triple bottom line include a company's relationships with multiple stakeholders as well as the natural environment. Measures need to be specifically developed to measure important processes, impacts and outcomes with respect to each stakeholder of significance, as well as the natural environment. For example:

7.3.1 Economic or primary stakeholders

Economic or primary stakeholders are the stakeholders without whom the business cannot exist. For example, owners, employees, suppliers and customers are stakeholders who have an economic 'stake' in companies.

- **Owners** make financial investments. In return for their investments, owners expect reasonable financial returns

- **Employees** and **labour unions** make intellectual and human capital investments. In return for their investments, employees and labour unions expect and deserve good working conditions, to be treated with respect and dignity, to be provided fair wages and benefits, fair and reasonable recruitment and retention policies, and good treatment by management, among other factors. That is, not only do employees expect that the basic labour standards embedded in International Labour Organisation conventions are met, but also, in many cases, that they are exceeded

- **Suppliers** can make economic and infrastructure investments that adapt to their customer companies' particular needs, and invest in developing trusting, loyal and long-term relationships with sourcing companies. In return for their investments, suppliers expect continued new business over time

● **Customers** invest their trust and their business (purchases). In return for their loyalty and business franchise, customers expect useful products and services that do no harm to them, their communities or the natural environment, that display the expected level of quality and that generally meet their needs

7.3.2 Societal or secondary stakeholders

Societal or secondary stakeholders are stakeholders affected by the ripple or secondary effects of the firm's activities: for example, communities, governmental officials, NGOs and activists, and civil-society organisations, such as schools, hospitals, social service agencies and religious institutions.

● **Communities** frequently make investments in infrastructure that enhance the company's ability to be productive. Infrastructure can include schools, hospitals, community services and activities, roads, sewers and water supplies, communication lines, and other amenities that make the community liveable and make it easier for companies to recruit and retain talented employees

● **Governments** can be local, state or provincial, regional and national. Governments invest in companies through tax and related incentives designed to bring business to an area; structure the rule of law that makes doing business feasible; and create the basic infrastructure needed for markets to work effectively and efficiently. In return for their investments, governments (at whatever level) provide the company with the necessary 'licence to operate' or social contract. Governments generally expect that companies will provide jobs to local residents at reasonable wages with reasonable benefits, be a source of economic development, pay reasonable taxes, and generally contribute to social welfare in an ongoing way. Additionally, governments that operate with integrity expect that companies will themselves operate with integrity, avoid corruption and be good corporate citizens by living up to their stated visions and values

- **NGOs and activists** typically have emotional and financial investments in changing certain behaviours and activities related to their particular interest area and hence need to be considered as relevant to a particular business. They are frequent critics of the corporation and can create demands and expectations for changed corporate behaviour that has fewer or different impacts and outcomes, depending on their arena of interest

- **Civil-society organisations** come in many forms. They can be linked to the interests of a particular business (e.g. a school that educates the local workforce) and hence are secondary stakeholders, or may not be stakeholders if they have a more remote relationship to the business. Civil-society organisations are, in many instances, linked only remotely to corporate activities; however, when they are connected, they expect to be treated as equal partners in a process of creating a civil society, to have their concerns heard and, within reason, acted on by the company

7.3.3 Environmental stakeholders

Nature or, as some ecologists say, Gaia (to mean the living planet) certainly has a stake in business activities, because nature supplies the raw materials needed to produce goods and services. The interests of the natural environment are typically represented by:

- **Activists and non-governmental organisations (NGOs)** specifically concerned about the environment, who have a stake in moving their cause or issue forward. Activists are frequently critical of corporate impacts and can make demands on companies that can seem unreasonable if there is no way for the company to engage with them to assess why they believe what they believe

● **Neighbours and communities** affected by firm activities that affect the environment, who have a stake in having a safe, healthy and clean environment in which to live and raise families. Neighbours and communities essentially provide the 'licence to operate' that many companies enjoy, and expect to be treated fairly and with respect in return

7.4 Criteria for measuring responsibility

The practices that companies evolve with respect to different stakeholders and the impacts that companies have on those stakeholders and the natural environment provide fruitful grounds for thinking about how to measure and assess the quality, impacts and nature of those relationships. In some respects, each company, because of the particular nature of its stakeholder and environmental relationships, needs to determine for itself (albeit often with the help of external consultants) what it is important to measure. What can be done, however, is to provide a way of thinking through how to measure what is frequently considered to be unmeasurable.

Measuring responsibility requires thinking through the costs and benefits of becoming more responsible towards stakeholders and the environment in ways that may not be immediately familiar. The GRI or Global Reporting Initiative has developed a number of principles that can help with such assessments. The GRI's principles are listed in Box 7.6.

7.5 Creating credibility in measurement

The principles above are intended to provide comprehensibility, scope of coverage and comparability across sustainability reports—or reports that cover economic, social and environmental issues, the well-known triple bottom line originally discussed by John Elkington. They are also

PRINCIPLES OF THE
GLOBAL REPORTING INITIATIVE

Transparency. Full disclosure of the processes, procedures and assumptions in report preparation are essential to its credibility.

Inclusiveness. The reporting organisation should systematically engage its stakeholders to help focus and continually enhance the quality of its reports.

Accountability. Reported data and information should be recorded, compiled, analysed and disclosed in a way that would enable internal auditors or external assurance providers to attest to its reliability.

Completeness. All information that is material to users for assessing the reporting organisation's economic, environmental and social performance should appear in the report in a manner consistent with the declared boundaries, scope and time period.

Relevance. Relevance is the degree of importance assigned to a particular aspect, indicator or piece of information, and represents the threshold at which information becomes significant enough to be reported.

Sustainability context. The reporting organisation should seek to place its performance in the larger context of ecological, social or other limits or constraints, where such context adds significant meaning to the reported information.

Accuracy. The accuracy principle refers to achieving the degree of exactness and low margin of error in reported information necessary for users to make decisions with a high degree of confidence.

Neutrality. Reports should avoid bias in selection and presentation of information and should strive to provide a balanced account of the reporting organisation's performance.

Comparability. The reporting organisations should maintain consistency in the boundary and scope of its reports, disclose any changes and re-state previously reported information.

Box 7.6 (continued over)

Source: GRI 2002

Clarity. The reporting organisation should remain cognisant of the diverse needs and backgrounds of its stakeholder groups and should make information available in a manner that is responsive to the maximum number of users while still maintaining a suitable level of detail.

Timeliness. Reports should provide information on a regular schedule that meets user needs and comports with the nature of the information itself.

Box 7.6 (from previous page)

meant to provide a degree of credibility to such reports that is lacking when the company simply issues the report using its own sense of what, when and how to report. As of late 2006, nearly 1,000 companies were registered in GRI's database and following its reporting guidelines.

Although not all companies developing responsibility management approaches use the GRI reporting methodologies, the GRI does represent a well-thought-out and organised *system* that can help companies begin to figure out what to measure and how to measure it. Another approach, undertaken jointly by SustainAbility and the United Nations Environment Programme, argues that companies can make the business case for responsibility by focusing on the intersection of ten measures of business success and ten dimensions of corporate sustainable development (see Table 7.1) (van Heel *et al.* 2001). Their matrix focuses specifically on the key areas of governance, general business, environment, socioeconomic performance and engagement.

TEN MEASURES OF BUSINESS SUCCESS	TEN DIMENSIONS OF CORPORATE SUSTAINABLE DEVELOPMENT PERFORMANCE
Financial performance 1. Shareholder value 2. Revenue 3. Operational efficiency 4. Access to capital **Financial drivers** 5. Customer attraction 6. Brand value and reputation 7. Human and intellectual capital 8. Risk profile 9. Innovation 10. Licence to operate	**Governance** 1. Ethics, values and principles 2. Accountability and transparency **General** 3. Triple-bottom-line commitment **Environment** 4. Environmental process focus 5. Environmental product focus **Socioeconomic** 6. Socioeconomic development 7. Human rights 8. Workplace conditions **Stakeholder engagement** 10. Engaging business partners 11. Engaging non-business partners

TABLE 7.1 Measures of business success and dimensions of corporate sustainable development performance

Source: van Heel *et al.* 2001

7.6 Thinking outside the box about measuring responsibility

Numerous systems for assessment of responsibility performance have cropped up in recent years and, at the time of writing, there is no accepted single standard. Thus, companies to date can choose the system of reporting that appeals to them. Many activists call into question the voluntary nature of many current initiatives. As a result, the more a company can abide by, for example, the general principles outlined above in the GRI, which is the best-established and most comprehensive existing framework, the better off they will be. Further, the more companies can make their reports available to relevant stakeholders in the interest of transparency and accountability, the more likely they are to benefit from the reputational advantages that accrue to companies seen to be progressive in managing their responsibilities effectively.

7.6.1 An example of costing out a problem area

Let us take a simple example that may help explain how to begin thinking about measuring for responsibility. Let us say that a company has poor employee relations. What are some of the possible costs of problems with employees? Well, for one thing, productivity could be diminished because employees are dissatisfied and not willing to give their all to the job; they may fail to offer suggestions that could improve the processes with which they are involved and therefore productivity. They may also have greater levels of absenteeism, turnover, tardiness and personal illnesses, all of which are costly to the company. By improving working conditions, pay, worker treatment, safety or employee relationships, the company may be able to gain measurable benefits with respect to productivity, employee turnover, recruitment and retention, and reduced absenteeism that greatly outweigh the costs associated with the improvements.

Some improvements can be of benefit and cost nothing. For example, managers can treat employees well and empower them to take charge of their own jobs at little financial cost yet, not surprisingly, find that employees respond positively to the respect they are offered and the dignity with which they are treated. Benefits to the firm may include more innovation and suggestions, employees assuming more responsibility for the quality of their work, greater loyalty, and a reduction in employee-related problems that cost managerial time. By thinking carefully about typically unaccounted costs such as recruitment costs, absenteeism and managerial time spent on problems, and creating measures to take the impact of positive changes into account, companies readily see the benefits of managing responsibility.[1]

Similar arguments can be made with respect to each of the relevant stakeholders. For instance, by making improvements in the quality system, companies can carry out more targeted and hence relevant research and development, which results in happier customers, who then purchase more of the company's goods and services, return products or complain less about services, and become repeat customers. Similarly, by reducing or eliminating waste, whether of materials or labour, companies can reduce their negative environmental impacts. In addition, they can reduce compliance and regulatory costs, as well as complaints by external activists, avoid reputational damage (which can trigger social investors to withdraw their investments) and sometimes reduce liabilities.[2] By carefully thinking through the costs associated with negative practices, as well as the systemic benefits of improvements, managers can begin to take a much more holistic perspective on the company's practices and impacts on stakeholders and the natural environment.

There are numerous organisations and initiatives that can help provide guidance to companies that wish to begin measuring—and improving on—the responsibility of their stakeholder relationships and, ultimately, triple bottom lines. Box 7.7 provides the names and websites of some of the organisations currently working on the development and implementation of responsibility assessment systems.

---

1   These examples are from Neil Smith of SmithOBrien, a firm in New York City, USA, that undertakes responsibility audits (see www.smithobrien. com).

2   www.smithobrien.com

A *SAMPLE* OF RESPONSIBILITY ASSESSMENT AND REPORTING TOOLS

GENERAL RESPONSIBILITY ASSESSMENTS

Global Reporting Initiative (GRI) is a multi-stakeholder, global initiative to develop, promote and disseminate a generally accepted framework for voluntary reporting of economic, environmental and social performance for organisations aimed at making sustainability reporting as routine and credible as financial reporting.

See: www.globalreporting.org

GENERAL STANDARDS AND PRINCIPLES

The Global Compact is a United Nations initiative that provides a set of ten voluntary principles in the areas of human rights, labour rights, the environment and anti-corruption to which companies agree to adhere in an effort to build sustainable economies.

See: www.unglobalcompact.org

Organisation for Economic Co-operation and Development (OECD) is a multi-stakeholder organisation that provides guidelines for multinational enterprises focusing on labour, environment, anti-corruption, fair business, technology transfer and sound operating principles.

See: www.oecd.org

The Global Sullivan Principles promote ethical business conduct on issues of human rights, labour, environment, sustainable development and anti-corruption.

See: www.globalsullivanprinciples.org/principles.htm

GENERAL RESPONSIBILITY ASSESSMENTS: INTERNAL

AccountAbility 1000 (AA1000) is a process-based standard that covers social accounting, auditing and reporting focused on the overall quality of dialogue and stakeholder participation.

See: www.accountability21.net

Box 7.7 (continued opposite)

Corporate responsibility audits: SmithOBrien provides cross-functional, internally oriented, value-added responsibility audits that can help prepare companies for external audit, or simply improve results.

See: www.smithobrien.com

SustainAbility's goal is to create a more sustainable world by encouraging the evolution and widespread adoption of thinking and practices that are economically competitive, environmentally sound and socially responsible, focused on the 'triple bottom line of sustainable development'.

See: www.sustainability.com

LABOUR STANDARDS AND WORKPLACE PRACTICE ASSESSMENTS

Social Accountability International: SA8000 is a voluntary international standard that attempts to assure ethical sourcing of goods and services.

See: www.sa-intl.org

Fair Labor Association (FLA) is a voluntary initiative of businesses and other stakeholders aimed at protecting labour rights, establishing a global code of conduct, and creating an independent monitoring system that holds companies publicly accountable for their labour practices. FLA accredits monitors, certifies compliance and serves as an information source.

See: www.fairlabor.org

ENVIRONMENTAL ASSESSMENTS

Coalition for Environmentally Responsible Economics (CERES) Principles. CERES builds networks of companies meeting its environmental principles, promotes environmental reporting including establishing reporting guidelines, and works closely with the GRI to create a framework for global sustainability reporting.

See: www.ceres.org

Box 7.7 (from previous page; continued over)

International Organisation for Standardisation (ISO), ISO 14000 and 14063 Series provide standard frameworks for assessing environmental (and related) management. ISO 26000 standards (guidance on social responsibility) are due in 2008.

See: www.iso.org

Box 7.7 (from previous page)

7.7 Transparency and accountability for results and impacts

Data from the responsibility measurement system are used to produce responsibility reports addressing internal and external practices and the impacts of corporate activities. Companies determine how to develop trust with external and internal stakeholders through dialogue and assure the validity and reliability of their accountability systems in a cost-effective way.

7.7.1 Internal/external assessment? Third-party monitoring and certification?

Many companies use a combination of both internal and external (third-party) assessment and monitoring to assess their responsibility management systems. External monitoring and sometimes certification of the audit process is sometimes considered necessary, particularly when a company has been under significant external pressures from critics about its employee or environmental practices in particular.

Internal assessment and monitoring is important as a management tool: it helps companies identify areas that need improvement or that might get them in trouble with different stakeholders if problems are not resolved. They use third-party monitors for several reasons. One reason is to build trust with their stakeholders and provide credibility for their responsibility management systems. A second reason for third-party assessment and monitoring is that some markets or businesses require it as part of their terms of engagement, as, for example, in the case of some of the major footwear companies who have now implemented such requirements from their suppliers. A third reason is that companies are serious about living up to their own or external standards and want to have assurance for themselves, as well as their stakeholders, that they are in reality as responsible as they claim to be.

Different stakeholders create different assessment and monitoring needs. For example, purchasing staff might be assessed, in their annual performance review, for their support of the company's code of conduct or the principles under which the company is said to operate, particularly in supply chains. Similarly, country managers might have the same expectations and conditions placed on them. Compliance personnel or, in some cases, entire buyer operations can be assessed, to ensure that the standards the company is signatory to are met. For example, some companies adhere to the Fair Labor Association (FLA) standards with respect to their supply chain manufacturers, and need to be reviewed every third year to ensure their compliance. FLA provides independent monitoring that helps to establish the credibility of the company's efforts to operate responsibly through their certification procedures.

INDICATORS

DELOITTE TOUCHE TOHMATSU: TRUST–BUILDING BROKERS

Third-party verification has proved to be one of the most challenging parts of implementation. This type of auditing includes a complex set of decisions for firms involving selection of auditors, selection of indicators and reporting results to stakeholders. This case describes an emerging alternative to external auditing.

Box 7.8 (continued over)

COMPANY HISTORY AND BACKGROUND

Deloitte Consulting is part of Deloitte Touche Tohmatsu, one of the world's largest professional services firms, providing consulting, assurance and advisory, and tax services to both public and private institutions in over 150 countries. Deloitte Consulting services extend to all aspects of enterprise transformation, such as strategy and processes, information technology, human resources and more recently corporate social responsibility (www.deloitte.com/dtt/section_home/0,1041,sid%253D1014,00.html, accessed December 2006).

FROM FINANCIAL TO ENVIRONMENTAL AND SOCIAL AUDITING

With a long history of consulting on business systems, in the early 1990s Deloitte began consulting to companies on environmental issues. Their consulting evolved to assess more than environmental management systems and came to include reporting on client performance related to internal and external stakeholders. Today these corporate social responsibility (CSR) services have expanded rapidly. They include a range of consulting services such as (1) making the business case—helping executives understand that CSR is valuable to corporation; (2) developing CSR strategies and policies; (3) developing organisational principles and measures to integrate them into an organisation; (4) monitoring and measuring of progress; (5) reporting and communicating to various stakeholder groups; and (6) verifying social information and reports.

AUDITING TO TRUST BUILDING

Deloitte believes that the last two categories—reporting to stakeholders and verifying social information—are interdependent activities. In the TRM model improvement and learning is predicated on providing transparency of the data and the collection process to stakeholders. Given that social information is often qualitatively oriented, verification becomes a much more complex process. Often activists and other members of civil society challenge internal company monitoring practices and social reporting on the grounds

Box 7.8 (from previous page; continued opposite)

that they lack transparency. Until recently some companies relied on consultant firms to perform third-party social audits because they were considered credible. However, another challenge is that many of these social reports, whether internally or externally produced, contain measures that are of lesser interest to external stakeholder groups while other more relevant measures to these civil-society groups are overlooked.

Noticing this mismatch between information collected by companies and information desired by stakeholders, Deloitte helped develop the practice of 'trust-building processes' as an alternative to third-party verification. This consists of having civil society approve of a company's 'soft' social information. Such a process often entails a series of events at which companies involve NGOs in assessing the credibility of corporate reporting. Deloitte consultants wear a number of hats when organising these types of stakeholder engagement process. First, consultants often assist companies with identifying key NGOs with which to hold their dialogues—stakeholder identification in TRM.

Second, in circumstances where experience with these types of collaboration is low for both the companies and NGO participants, consultants help facilitate dialogues between these groups on challenging topics. This typifies the best type of TRM stakeholder engagement—those that are efficient, broad, provide depth and gather new information about what stakeholders want.

Third, Deloitte consultants help companies communicate with stakeholders not just through reports, but targeted communications that deliver information that meets the needs of stakeholder groups. This final role is a core element of the 'trust building' alternative and is indeed a good example of the TRM aspect, reporting to stakeholders, which requires the provision of transparent and meaningful information.

Since auditors have trust from both the corporate and NGO community, they have the opportunity by bringing together both audiences to define the necessary social responsibility measures for the company to report. This results in corporations generating and reporting a much more purposeful amount of information aimed at

Box 7.8 (from previous page; continued over)

key stakeholders. Once these measures are determined, external auditors can still be involved in verifying quantitative information assessing various CSR measures by examining internal company documents. With the qualitative measures a stakeholder group then interprets and comments on the information. The second step is aimed at helping build credibility and trust around information.

The verification process can take many forms. Often it consists of creating an advisory board with other NGOs, stakeholders and corporate executives. When the previously agreed measures are subsequently reported, the advisory board can then verify that they have been informed and state that the group is comfortable that the report is true, correct or in accordance to their wishes. The verification step can go beyond simply NGO approval of the information. Some companies are inviting NGOs to visit their sites or projects in question, another practice exemplifying the TRM ideal. In the situation of multinational corporations working in a number of countries, local NGOs conduct visits to gather information and report to headquarters or partnering NGOs that their needs have been satisfied. More open trust-building processes can include the stakeholder sounding board: freely asking for information on different issues and issuing a statement that the information given is sufficient. Most often, operational-level managers report the information identified as relevant to the advisory board. The interpretation of information is the job of the advisory board where corporate executives are also represented.

EMERGING PRACTICE

Deloitte anticipates the future of stakeholder relations communication moving into strong NGO involvement, as well as employee involvement. Information is no longer given by the company but is an exchange between key actors to determine the relevant details and interpret them. Although Deloitte could not provide specific numbers, they believe that these types of 'trust-building' process are an emerging trend being used by high-profile corporations, with others following in their tracks.

Box 7.8 (from previous page; continued opposite)

CHALLENGES

The first challenge is to make corporations and stakeholders meet and trust in the process. Second, it is difficult initially to have stakeholders understand that, to the extent they receive information, it is confidential. Third, securing board of directors commitment can be an initial obstacle since resistance to these new types of engagement is common.

LESSONS LEARNED BY DELOITTE IN TRUST–BUILDING PROCESSES

Stakeholder learning. From these exchanges, all the stakeholders learn about the concerns and agendas of their various counterparts. Part of this includes business and stakeholders developing an understanding of each other's expectations for ways of working together and the dilemmas corporations face.

Knowledge sharing. From the corporate perspective, they gain useful knowledge in these trust–building activities from the expertise of NGOs who have considerable experience working on CSR issues. Furthermore, both corporations and civil society can co–operate and solve problems using their strengths in unison.

Top–management commitment. Critical to these exchanges are setting the scene and having top–management commitment from all parties. For corporations, board of directors approval for trying this process out is fundamental. Often directors are reluctant in the beginning since trust–building activities are a new way to engage with society, but when they see positive results such as knowledge sharing their attitudes become more positive.

Third–party facilitation. Using external management firms to convene trust–building exchanges can provide the initial steps needed to build trust between business and its external stakeholders.

Box 7.8 (from previous page)

8

Getting started

CHANGE MANAGEMENT AND THE COMPLEXITY OF BEING 'GLOCAL'

So . . . how do you begin moving your company towards managing responsibility explicitly if it is not already doing so? Or make that approach more systemic if your company has already begun this process? There are several keys to designing and implementing a company-specific TRM system:

- Remember that implementing responsibility management is, like quality management, a long-term and ongoing process. TRM is more like a journey than an end-point

- Understand that TRM requires a process of organisational change, development and evolution that pays attention to all of the company's stakeholders, particularly internal stakeholders such as employees who are involved in and need to be committed to the responsibility management process

- Top management needs to be committed to the *vision* and *processes* involved in responsibility management, work to establish a *shared* vision for managing responsibility throughout the organisation, and work hard to ensure that responsibility for responsibility is devolved throughout the organisation. Everyone needs to be 'bought in' to responsibility management

● Improvement, innovation and feedback are critical components of responsibility management. To be successful in the improvement process, leaders throughout the organisation (whether in formal positions of power or not) need to figure out how to measure responsibility, provide baseline and improvement data to those who can make improvements, and allow for mistakes

As must be clear, managing responsibilities inevitably requires significant organisational and system transformation and change. But the rewards and benefits of managing more responsibly accrue not only to the multiple bottom lines associated with different stakeholders and the natural environment, but also to the company as a whole through enhancement of the company's reputation.

TRM approaches provide a *framework* for action and change that moves a company's practices towards continual improvement of stakeholder relationships and better use of natural resources. TRM approaches suggest ways for managers and leaders to consider how to integrate responsibility into company *systems* making the company's corporate citizenship real, not just rhetoric. The company's internal operating systems need to be matched to its strategies, goals and culture: that is, inspiration or vision and outcomes need to be brought into alignment via operating practices and management systems. The TRM framework's four main components encompass the major elements that need to be considered in managing responsibility:

● Inspiration

● Integration

● Innovations and improvements, plus indicators

Responsibility management is about taking a systemic perspective on what *impacts* a firm's activities have, including implementation of its responsibility objectives. When there are problems, responsibility management is about adjusting cross-organisational processes accordingly. Responsibility management is thus dependent on modifying existing strategies, operating practices and relationships so that they are aligned with the company's stated vision and values and can be communicated effectively to a wide range of stakeholders. The inspirational elements of TRM work best if they support the company's integrity, values-driven vision and stakeholder relationships that *honour* the perspectives that different stakeholders affected by the company's business activities bring to company decisions and impacts.

8.1 TRM: continual change and improvement

Obviously, for many companies, adopting a responsibility management system means thinking through the company's vision, values and systems in a way that may not have been consciously attended to before. Such a shift implies a significant organisational transformation in many cases, just as the shift to quality management implied total organisational change to incorporate quality considerations in all that the company did. So too with responsibility management: the decision to manage responsibility involves the whole enterprise and its stakeholders, particularly the employees who will be responsible for implementation and the development and maintenance of stakeholder relationships.

John Kotter, who studies organisational transformation, suggests that there are eight key steps involved in successful organisational transformation. In Box 8.1 we adapt Kotter's framework to responsibility management systems (Kotter 1995: 61). Missing any one of these important steps can, according to Kotter, cause the change effort to fail.

Box 8.2 illustrates one company's integrative approach to total responsibility management.

EIGHT STEPS TO TRANSFORMING ORGANISATIONS THROUGH TRM

1. ESTABLISH A SENSE OF URGENCY

Evaluate and diagnose the need for responsibility management by assessing stakeholder demands and expectations and particularly by engaging with important stakeholders. Look externally at critics, the media, governments and NGO activists to see where problems are perceived. Look internally at employee participation, employment and working conditions to see where problems exist.

Identify and create dialogue internally and externally about the reputational and competitive impacts of a stakeholder or environmental crisis, focusing on potential threats and crises as well as major opportunities for competitive advantage.

2. FORM A POWERFUL GUIDING COALITION

Assemble a group of allies who are able and willing to lead the change effort, who understand the need for responsibility management, quality management and good stakeholder relationships. Draw this group from a wide range of functions in the organisation, particularly tapping into those who regularly deal with internal stakeholders (employees and labour unions, in particular) and external stakeholders, both friendly to the firm and unfriendly.

Arrange team-building activities that break down barriers that might exist among members of the coalition so that its members can work together as a team.

3. CREATE A VISION THAT EMBEDS RESPONSIBILITY AND VALUES

Create an inspirational and aspirational vision around responsibility management and the goal of the company that draws stakeholders in and helps guide decision-making, being sure to articulate the company's core values.

Box 8.1 (continued over)

Source: adapted from Kotter 1995

Ensure that the guiding coalition serves as a role model for the rest of the members of the company as well as stakeholders who may be observing the company.

4. COMMUNICATE THE VISION

Develop numerous and frequent communication modalities for communicating the new vision and strategies intended to achieve it.

Have top management constantly reinforce the need for responsibility management and the company's core values.

Use the guiding coalition and other stakeholders as role models and exemplars for implementing the responsibility vision.

5. EMPOWER OTHERS TO ACT ON THE VISION

Diagnose obstacles to change and provide means of removing them.

Change important systems so that they are supportive of the new vision and goals, paying particular attention to: reward systems, information systems, communication systems, and employee-related systems and benefits.

Encourage internal stakeholders to take risks, generate innovations and implement new ideas and activities.

6. PLAN FOR AND CREATE SHORT-TERM WINS

Plan and implement short-term and visible improvements. Communicate them widely.

Recognise and reward employees who are making improvements.

Assess supply chain management, purchasing processes, production and operations, marketing, distribution and human resource systems, as well as other relevant internal systems, to provide a baseline, then institute measures to determine whether and where improvements are needed.

7. CONSOLIDATE IMPROVEMENTS AND PRODUCE MORE CHANGE

Once credible change has been established, use the credibility it generates to eliminate systems, structures and policies that are not responsible or don't match the company's stated values. Continue to

Box 8.1 (from previous page; continued opposite)

measure stakeholder and ecological performance and communicate results transparently to relevant parties.

Hire, reward, promote and recognise with development, training and promotions employees who institute positive changes.

Reinvigorate the process periodically with new projects, people and practices.

8. INSTITUTIONALISE NEW APPROACHES

Make the links between performance and the responsibility management approaches that have been adopted.

Develop new means to ensure that leaders emerge from within the ranks of current employees.

Box 8.1 (from previous page)

INTEGRATION

A TRM APPROACH:
SAINSBURY'S: SUPPLY CHAIN MANAGEMENT*

We have around 2,500 immediate contract suppliers, but we now like to talk in terms of having a complex supplier web—since it is continuously changing (Socially Responsible Trading Manager).

Mass-market retailers often face the situation of having hundreds, even thousands of suppliers. As retail firms continue to outsource production and simultaneously face consumer pressure to act socially and environmentally responsibly, supply chain management requires consideration of cost and quality, as well as labour and environmental management. This case details how Sainsbury's, a leading UK grocer with over 30,000 products, has developed management systems that support its vision of ethical conduct and assessment processes that allow for learning and change.

A SOURCING DILEMMA

The founders' principles and values appear to guide the company as strongly today as they did at the outset, as summarised in one of its primary goals:

> At Sainsbury's we will deliver an ever-improving quality shopping experience for our customers with great products at fair prices. We will exceed customers' expectations for healthy, safe, fresh and tasty food, making their lives easier every day (www.j-sainsbury.com/files/reports/cr2006/files/report.pdf, accessed December 2006).

---

* Much of this case is also used in Waddock and Leigh 2006.

Box 8.2 (continued opposite)

Sources: www.sainsburys.com, accessed December 2006; home page: www.j-sainsbury.co.uk; corporate social responsibility page: www.sainsburys.co.uk/social, accessed August 2003; www.hoovers.com/j-sainsbury/--ID__40427--/free-co-factsheet.xhtml, accessed December 2006; www.j-sainsbury.co.uk/index.asp?pageid=204, accessed December 2006; Ethical Trading Initiative: www.ethicaltrade.org; Fairtrade: www.fairtrade.org.uk

What do you do if you are a company with over 1,400 immediate suppliers? What do you do if these suppliers source from 50–100 countries around the world? In a world of long and complex supply chains, when does a company determine when it becomes 'responsible' for the working and environmental conditions under which its sourced product is produced? These are the types of question that Sainsbury's contends with on a regular basis.

Sainsbury's 'attention to detail' now includes fundamental questions about product sourcing. Two examples highlight the challenges in this domain. For instance, consumption goods such as chocolate do not immediately draw suspicion since the actual chocolate producers, predominantly located in the western European countries, meet internationally recognised standards. However, the actual suppliers of cocoa (one of the main ingredients in chocolate) to the manufacturers are, in some instances, highly suspect in terms of violations of child labour laws. This is because cocoa is a commodity product harvested in African countries and sourced through subcontractors where it is difficult to monitor each individual farm.

Another example of this type of challenge is with non-food products, such as the toys in Christmas crackers. Many of the toys in Sainsbury's crackers are sourced by importing houses in Hong Kong, from numerous factories in China, many of which use subcontractors. The complex contracting arrangements compounded by China's history of various human rights violations, such as the use of forced and prison labour, makes it difficult for Sainsbury's to assess actual working conditions.

These types of situation and many others like them have sparked an internal debate on the question: at what step does the product become Sainsbury's? More specifically, at what point does the company become responsible for the ethical and environmental consequences of its production? Before discussing Sainsbury's response to these questions we present an overview of the company and background to its CSR initiatives.

Box 8.2 (from previous page; continued over)

COMPANY HISTORY AND CSR BACKGROUND

Sainsbury's Supermarket was established in 1869 by John James and Mary Ann Sainsbury and is Britain's longest-standing major food retailing chain. It is held by parent company J Sainsbury and is the UK's third-largest food retailer (after Tesco and ASDA) with 752 stores. Over 30,000 products are stocked, of which 50% are Sainsbury's own brand.

Starting in 1997, the company began developing initiatives for socially responsible sourcing for their brand food and non-food suppliers. Sainsbury's interest in these issues is reflected in the fact that it was a founding member of the ETI (Ethical Trading Initiative), a UK based cross-sectoral partnership of union, business and NGOs dedicated to promoting fair labour practices. In early 1998, the company established a Code of Practice on Socially Responsible Sourcing and has since issued it to all its brand suppliers. After establishing the Code of Practice, Sainsbury's began visiting its suppliers to raise both awareness of the code, and associated issues relating to ethical sourcing. Currently, the company is pursuing a number of specific projects with ETI, evaluating opportunities for independent monitoring of supplier compliance with the principles of the Code, and stocking a number of Fairtrade-certified products (an NGO dedicated to promoting fair labour and small business development). In this case we will examine Sainsbury's policies and practices through the lens of total responsibility management. TRM is a holistic model of corporate social and environmental responsibility divided into four components: inspiration, integration, innovation and indicators. Each of these components will be highlighted through the case.

INSPIRATION

[W]e are an international business, and our buyers source products from all over the world in order to provide the range of goods that we stock instore to meet the demands of our customers. This includes a number of developing countries where historically conditions for workers have been known to be poor (www.j-sainsburys.co.uk/cr/index.asp?pageid= 21&section=responsibility&subsection=suppliers&question=8).

Box 8.2 (from previous page; continued opposite)

The two key processes in the inspiration element of TRM are **vision setting**, answering the question 'What do we stand for?' and **leadership systems** that identify, communicate and support the vision. This requires a stakeholder engagement process that determines the key stakeholders in the responsibility vision and develops dialogue, communication and mutuality with important stakeholders to inform operating practices. Evidence of stakeholder awareness is seen in the web statement on Sainsbury's involvement in ethical trade: Sainsbury's became 'involved in this area [because] [i]t became apparent over time that the subject of socially responsible sourcing was a growing area of concern for ourselves as a Company and our customers'.

Ethical trading is a big component of the company's CSR initiatives, which it considers to include a broad number of areas: the environment, organics, genetic modification, product safety, animal welfare, and the welfare and human rights of workers and their labour conditions. The Code of Conduct focuses on the last of these CSR initiatives identified above related to human rights and labour. These concentrate on four main areas: (1) protection of children, (2) health and safety, (3) equal opportunities, (4) freedom of association and remuneration (see www.j-sainsburys.com/files/reports/cr2006/files/sis_code.pdf, accessed December 2006). The Code of Conduct provides a vision for detailing the company's supplier relationships and is also a requirement for its participation in ETI.

Besides virtual communication strategies, the company demonstrates its leadership commitment to its CSR activities through CEO and board-level endorsement of the Code of Conduct. In fact, when Peter Davis took over as CEO in 2000 the CSR group made sure the new leadership backed the initiatives supporting the vision, as well as the vision itself. When the group presented the activities to Davis, he offered his commitment, asked for a presentation to the board and provided a budget for further activities. Justin King, appointed CEO in 2004, continued the trend of top-leadership endorsement of the company's CSR initiatives.

Box 8.2 (from previous page; continued over)

INTEGRATION: TRANSLATING CSR PRINCIPLES

Integration of 'responsibility' into all relevant management systems requires a clear strategy and supportive human resource practices. This section examines these components of Sainsbury's efforts to build responsibility into the business. We first turn to its strategy.

Strategy
Sainsbury's strategy focus for achieving its vision, leadership and corporate goals in responsibilities areas depends on a five-tiered approach.

1. Monitoring of name-brand suppliers (discussed in more detail below)
2. External collaborations with the ETI for knowledge sharing
3. Commitment to fair-trade products
4. Communication of policies and practices internally and externally
5. Special projects: focusing on certain areas with collaborating organisations—for example, learning more about child labour in supply chains and initiatives to reduce working hours in India and China

All of these policies require extensive human resource changes since it is ultimately employees who implement a company's vision. These adjustments in human resource activities can include job design, training, performance appraisal, recruitment, employee development, communication and empowerment practices in order to be in alignment with this vision. Sainsbury's efforts to address a number of these human resource components through organisational structure changes, job responsibilities and training are reviewed below.

Organisational structure and responsibility: CSR team
In order to actively implement its ethical trading activities Sainsbury's needed to amend its organisational structure. Beginning in November 2000 Sainsbury's assigned a full-time person—the Socially Responsible Trading (SRT) Manager—to be responsible for co-ordinating its ethical trading activities. The first of these activities involves working with and training product managers, the company's

Box 8.2 (from previous page; continued opposite)

principal interface with the supply base. Another major task of this position requires managing the ethical side of supplier relationships. This includes ensuring that all new suppliers are contacted in order to inform them of Sainsbury's objectives, obtaining their commitment to achieving these, and maintaining the database detailing current suppliers and their progress to date on compliance with the code. In addition, the SRT Manager works with the commercial departments to balance the capacity of the suppliers to make necessary changes while maintaining competitiveness.

JOB DESIGN: AUDITING

Sainsbury's has two types of internal auditor at present, technical and ethical. The existence of the first, technical auditing, is not surprising given Sainsbury's line of business. The technologists monitor supplier operations by visiting production sites. This built-in structure is due partially to the legal quality requirements necessary to evaluate domestic goods and foreign imports, as well as Sainsbury's founding vision. Given that it is already visiting supplier sites, the company decided to build small aspects of the ethical criteria into its regular auditing process. In addition, an ethical auditing function was developed to evaluate the implementation of the Code of Conduct. The ethical auditors and technologists maintain regular contact to relay critical information. An in-depth description of the monitoring process follows in the Innovation section below.

One instance of this collaboration is when a technologist is scheduled to visit a supplier site that had been identified with problems in the preceding months by the ethical auditors. With an understanding of the problem and the agreed steps that the supplier has committed to in consultation with the ethical auditors, the technologist can check on progress and report back. This allows the company to relay a consistent and integrated message to suppliers and capitalise on the pre-existing design of job responsibilities.

Box 8.2 (from previous page; continued over)

Internal training

The company has developed two types of training, one for internal and another for external stakeholders. Internal training has focused on providing the technologists with appropriate information to evaluate basic elements of ethical performance. The second type of internal training by the SRT managers provide product managers with the necessary information and skills required to ensure that effective monitoring is carried out. As of 2002 all technical colleagues had received training (www.j-sainsbury.co.uk/files/pdf/eti_2003.pdf, accessed December 2006). The product managers' training includes an overview of the Code of Practice, an explanation of the contents, training on how these may be assessed during a visit, the areas that need to be included in the visit, and highlighting those areas where assessment may prove difficult. The company supplements these sessions with information packs on many of the countries it visits to provide background information. This training is crucial since product managers have the authority to both refuse to engage new suppliers following factory assessments that reveal inadequate practices, or limit further business with an existing supplier if significant issues are identified on a visit, and not resolved adequately. In the future, these types of structured and self-directed training are expected to expand by including more information on relevant local issues relating to the Code.

External training

In order to support the continuous improvement philosophy that guides supplier relationships, Sainsbury's has begun to offer specialised training to this external stakeholder. In February 2001, Sainsbury's organised a conference on gang labour in the UK using illegal workers. By teaming up with immigration officials and Home Office staff, the conference was designed to teach UK agricultural suppliers about this specific aspect of the ethical aims. Some of the supplier feedback from this training stated that they are now able to see what they can do within their own system and viewed the training as a catalyst. During 2005 Sainsbury's organised a number of free workshops for gangmasters to help them meet the new legal requirements beginning in 2005/2006 (www.j-sainsbury.com/files/reports/cr2006/files/report.pdf, accessed December 2006).

Box 8.2 (from previous page; continued opposite)

Training needs to be supplemented by a system that actually measures what is going on within the company.

INNOVATIONS, IMPROVEMENTS AND INDICATORS

TRM approaches indicate that, in order to achieve progress towards the responsibility vision, three major mechanisms are needed: (1) strategies that promote transparency and accountability for results; (2) tactics that foster improvement, remediation and learning; and (3) a measurement system that assesses performance on social, environmental and financial criteria. Sainsbury's approach to each of these areas will be discussed in turn.

INTERNAL AND EXTERNAL COMMUNICATION THAT PROMOTE TRANSPARENCY AND ACCOUNTABILITY

The external challenge is letting people know what we are doing and explain the complexity of it all (Liz Fullelove, Socially Responsible Trading Manager, 2001).

In order to share information internally there is a formal quarterly review of progress, which involves the chief executive and commercial director. In addition, monthly meetings are conducted with senior managers within the technical division, where socially responsible sourcing has become a formal agenda item. Also, the company has used its internal magazine, which is circulated to all employees. Starting in 2000, external communication of activities occurs through formal company presentations at a number of conferences such as the Council For Economic Priorities, Oxfam, Pensions, Investment, Research Consultants Ltd, and the International Produce Consortium. Over the past few years the company has developed an extensive internet site to enable wider access by customers and suppliers to information on current activities within the CSR area. All of these internal, conference and digital venues support the distribution of critical CSR information and signal the company's dedication to transparency and accountability with multiple stakeholders.

Box 8.2 (from previous page; continued over)

TARGET GOALS AND MONITORING TO PROMOTE IMPROVEMENT, REMEDIATION AND LEARNING

Sustaining improvement requires the careful design of responsibility objectives for each of the company's core stakeholders and tracking of those goals. Sainsbury's illustrates this through setting priorities and targets for the next year. As of October 2001 it has defined its main concerns as follows.

All new suppliers agree to the terms of Sainsbury's Code of Practice as part of the business relationship (for more details on current CSR activities, see www.j-sainsbury.com/files/reports/cr2006/files/srs_code.pdf, accessed December 2006). Further, all outstanding high- and medium-risk suppliers are periodically visited and training has been expanded to the commercial departments to secure their engagement in progressing the initiative. This move involves up to 300 personnel. In addition to providing the basic training for all 28 outstanding product managers, further training of all product managers is being developed, in order to provide additional help and advice for visits, to improve the level and capability of monitoring. Findings of the third-party agency inspections are evaluated to identify an appropriate route to use these to help facilitate implementation of satisfactory standards if necessary. The company also intends to expand the internet site in order to facilitate the wider communication of Sainsbury's position and activities. In addition, other methods for providing broader communication with customers are being investigated. Further, there are plans to incorporate the Homebase suppliers within the current database, in order to monitor progress made by both companies.

Besides these efforts the company has committed to a number of specific initiatives that support their responsibility goals. In their own words,

> In addition to involvement with two of the ETI pilot schemes in South Africa and Zimbabwe, Sainsbury's will be involved in the 4th ETI project in Costa Rica. In addition, Sainsbury's are funding £25,000 towards an initiative in South Africa to help support a training programme to provide entrepreneurial training for Cape

Box 8.2 (from previous page; continued opposite)

women to enable them to set up a small business. It is planned that Sainsbury's will help to market the final products manufactured by the women, and identify a potential mechanism for their sale.

We have also started to have an involvement in specific projects. For example, in conjunction with one of our suppliers, Capespan, we have been involved in sponsoring some training programmes for women in South Africa in order to provide them with the business skills they need to help obtain financial independence. We are considering future opportunities for involvement in other projects where we can help make a difference to workers on a day to day basis (www.sainsburys.co.uk/social, accessed August 2003).

AUDITING SYSTEMS AS AN ELEMENT OF RESPONSIBILITY MEASUREMENT SYSTEM

Supported by the ETI Base Code (which is based on ILO Conventions), [the Code of Conduct principles] are an expression of the social values we share with our partner companies and provide a basis for our trading relationships (www.j-sainsbury.com/files/reports/cr2006/files/srs_code.pdf, accessed December 2006).

SUPPLIER PHILOSOPHY

Sainsbury's engagement philosophy is summarised in its 2006 Socially Responsible Sourcing Report as follows:

If we find an issue, it is discussed fully with the supplier, in order to understand its implications and to find the best solution for addressing it.

Our philosophy is not to pull out of a factory if issues are found. Whilst this would help protect the Sainsbury's name and reputation, it does not ultimately help the conditions and welfare of the workers. If, for example, we were to take our

Box 8.2 (from previous page; continued over)

business suddenly away from a factory where we were a major customer, this could have a detrimental effect on the factory, and could lead to closure or loss of jobs. This is not how we wish to operate, as we want to work to protect the workers and improve their conditions.

Instead, we discuss with the factory the opportunity for a continuous improvement programme. The supplier would then advise us of the actions they plan to take and the timescales involved. If for example a new accommodation block is required, this will involve time and money and cannot be expected to happen overnight. However, we would agree a programme with the supplier for these changes to occur and would monitor the improvements made.

However, if over time the supplier consistently fails to demonstrate a commitment to meeting the principles of the code and improving the conditions for their workers, and does not wish to work in partnership with us, then of course we would review the conditions and status of their trading relationship with us (www.sainsburys.co.uk/social, accessed August 2002).

From these supplier audits, a number of issues have begun to emerge. These include:

1. Language barriers: especially in the absence of an interpreter or representative

2. Time limitations of product managers when assessing both the technical and social aspects. This has resulted in either fewer areas covered or all areas covered in less detail

3. Obtaining information from staff, on occasion, has proved difficult, particularly if they are not used to being interviewed by visitors

4. Assessing compliance level has been difficult in some areas where there remain disputes locally as to what are acceptable standards (e.g. minimum wages in South Africa) (based on interview with Liz Fullelove, Socially Responsible Trading Manager, August 2002)

Box 8.2 (from previous page; continued opposite)

Types of auditing

Sainsbury's considers the assessment of current suppliers against the Code of Practice auditing process. Availability of records and full access to premises and staff will be important in demonstrating compliance.

Sainsbury's hierarchy for monitoring is as follows:

- Self-assessments by suppliers (low risk)
- Visits by quality managers/quality assurance managers (medium and high risk)
- External audits (medium and high risk)
- Multi-stakeholder monitoring (through ETI pilots)
- Working with industry to tackle industry-wide issues: e.g. commodities such as cocoa and coffee (www.j-sainsbury.com/files/pdf/eti_2003.pdf, accessed December 2006)

Third-party monitoring. During 2003 nine independent third-party inspections were carried out in order to make initial assessments of their capacity to monitor against the JS Code of Practice. The suppliers were selected to evaluate the effectiveness of third-party agencies. From the suppliers selected, it was anticipated that the management styles operating would generate high standards of socially responsible sourcing within their sector and country. A variety of approaches have been taken to date. In some circumstances, it was appropriate to focus in depth on a small number of areas. On some visits, all the criteria were discussed, but not necessarily in great depth. Some visits involved assessing compliance to the code by review and discussion of a self-assessment questionnaire completed by the supplier in advance of the visit.

There are several other dimensions to Sainsbury's auditing system ranging from risk assessment to self-assessment to supplementary technologist assessments to one-day ethical audits.

Risk assessment. This began in 1999 when Sainsbury's conducted an initial risk assessment exercise where suppliers were graded as high, medium and low risk. These assessments were not full compliance audits, but were based on a number of criteria such as country of

Box 8.2 (from previous page; continued over)

origin, whether suppliers had been visited previously, level of management commitment, whether undesirable social aspects were likely, and risk of media exposure. The 'high-risk suppliers' (80 at the time of initial assessment) were to be visited by the end of the financial year, in order that aspects of socially responsible sourcing could be discussed. Ninety-seven high-risk suppliers and 75 medium-risk suppliers were visited during the first year. In 2003, 25% of Sainsbury's 264 medium- and high-risk suppliers had received an external audit in the last two years. Besides assessing risk, '[t]he aim of their visits at this stage is to start to raise the awareness of socially responsible sourcing and the JS Code of Practice, and to begin to examine the associated issues' (www.sainsburys.co.uk/social, accessed August 2003). 'When issues are identified, the aim is to work with those suppliers towards achieving the standards expected whilst maintaining the security of continuing business'. Although the aspiration is to build relationships with possible suppliers, if they show evidence of major concern in Code of Practice areas, relationships are not pursued. It is also important to note that a number of these suppliers' risk classification has been re-categorised based on expanding knowledge and understanding of suppliers and issues.

Code of Practice. The first item companies are typically evaluated on is having a signed copy of their Code of Practice for suppliers at the facilities. The Code of Practice sets out how the Principles, which of necessity are described in general terms, can be applied in the ordinary course of business by both Sainsbury's and its suppliers. As of October 2001 Sainsbury's 1,117 brand suppliers (companies that produce goods that carry the Sainsbury's label) had been sent a copy of the Code of Practice, an accompanying letter from the Sainsbury Group Chief Executive, and a reply slip to confirm commitment to the principles of socially responsible sourcing. Replies were received from 773 (70%) suppliers, and a target has been set for all those outstanding to have done so by the end of the financial year.

Technologist audits. Sainsbury's brand products are produced to a detailed technical specification and they routinely monitor product quality and factory facilities with the staff of around 100 technologists.

Box 8.2 (from previous page; continued opposite)

As discussed in the Integration section, the technologist assessments provide the opportunity for the extensive technologist staff to provide reminders about social, labour and environmental issues after the ethical auditor visits. The technologists can follow up on or provide a few action points based on their findings. This is advantageous since the technologists can build on pre-existing relationships.

One-day ethical audits. Prior to implementing ethical audits, Sainsbury's tested full social audits but found that external auditors were stronger in some sectors than in others and varied by country. The company now uses full audits if necessary, but has developed an abbreviated audit which balances cost and time considerations. These one-day audits, run by an external agency, start with health and safety issues aimed at identifying the largest gaps and developing action plans (interview with Liz Fullelove, August 2002).

Measurement. During the internal ethical audits suppliers are ranked on a number of measures using a 0–4 scale. Those '0' scores represent scores given to factories where there is not compliance on an issue. Scores of '1' are considered poor, '2' progress needed, '3' satisfactory and '4' good.

WHAT DO YOU DO IF YOU ARE A COMPANY WITH OVER 1,400 IMMEDIATE SUPPLIERS?

> We have become more conscious of the need to take some share of the responsibility for social development, and for the welfare of employees who produce the goods we sell (www.sainsburys.co.uk/social, accessed August 2003)

A lot, if you are Sainsbury's. What do you do if these suppliers source from 50–100 countries around the world? Among many things, adopt a continuous improvement philosophy. Finally, in a world of long and complex supply chains, when does a company determine when it becomes 'responsible' for the working and environmental conditions under which its sourced product is produced? The answer to this complex question lies within the auditing practices. At this point,

Box 8.2 (from previous page; continued over)

Sainsbury's expects to audit ethical issues as far back as they would routinely audit. For example, with produce the company would visit the 'packhouse' (the supplier that consolidates the goods from numerous local farms), as well as a sample of farms that supply to the packhouse.

Box 8.2 (from previous page)

The Sainsbury's case illustrates not only the complexity but also the potential benefits of implementing a responsibility management system. Fewer surprises, better detailed information about *all* of the company's operations, and significantly less risk of reputational and performance problems are some of the benefits of taking such a systemic approach to managing not just some but all of the company's responsibilities explicitly and openly.

References

Adler, P.S., and R.E. Cole (1993) 'Designed for Learning: A Tale of Two Auto Plants', *Sloan Management Review* 35.3 (Spring 1993): 85-94.

Argyris, C. (1993) *Knowledge for Action: A Guide to Overcoming Barriers to Organizational Change* (San Francisco: Jossey Bass).

Byrne, J.A. (2000) 'Visionary vs. Visionary', in 'The 21st Century Corporation', *Business Week*, 21–28 August 2000: 210-12.

Chandler, A. (1962) *Strategy and Structure* (Cambridge, MA: MIT Press).

Clarkson, M.B.E. (1995) 'A Stakeholder Framework for Analyzing and Evaluating Corporate Social Performance', *Academy of Management Review* 20.1: 92-117.

Collins, J.C., and J.I. Porras (1997) *Built to Last: Successful Habits of Visionary Companies* (New York: HarperBusiness).

Cushman, D.P., and S.S. King (1997) *Continuously Improving an Organization's Performance: High-Speed Management* (New York: SUNY).

Deming, W.E. (1986) *Out of the Crisis* (Cambridge, MA: MIT Center for Advanced Educational Services).

Drucker, P. (1970) 'Entrepreneurship in Small Business', *Journal of Business Policy* 1.1: 3-12.

Economist (2001) 'Who's wearing the trousers?', *The Economist*, 8 September 2001.

Eizengerg, M.I., D.M. Gallo, I. Hagenbuch and A.N. Hoffman (2001) 'Cisco Systems, Inc.', in M.A. Hitt, R.D. Ireland and R.E. Hoskisson (eds.), *Strategic Management: Competitiveness and Globalization* (Belmont, CA: Southwestern Publishing, 4th edn).

Elkington, J. (1998) *Cannibals with Forks: The Triple Bottom Line of Sustainability* (Gabriola Island, Canada: New Society Publishers).

Freeman, R.E. (1984) *Strategic Management: A Stakeholder Approach* (Boston, MA: Pitman).

—— and D.R. Gilbert, Jr (1988) *Corporate Strategy and the Search for Ethics* (Englewood Cliffs, NJ: Prentice Hall).

——, J. Harrison and A. Wicker (2007) *Managing for Stakeholders: Business in the 21st Century* (New Haven, CT: Yale University Press).

GRI (Global Reporting Initiative) (2002) 'Global Reporting Initiative: Sustainability Reporting Guideline', www.globalreporting.org/guidelines/2002/gri_2002_guidelines.pdf, accessed October 2004.

Hartman, L.P., G. Arnold and R.E. Wokutch (2001) *Rising above Sweatshops: Innovative Approaches to Global Labor Challenges* (Westport, CT: Praeger).

Huselid, M.A. (1995) 'The Impact of Human Resource Management Practices on Turnover, Productivity, and Corporate Financial Performance', *Academy of Management Journal* 38: 647-72.

——, S.E. Jackson and R.S. Schuler (1997) 'Technical and Strategic Human Resource Management Effectiveness as Determinants of Firm Performance', *Academy of Management Journal* 40.1: 171-88.

Kotter, J.P. (1995) 'Leading Change: Why Transformation Efforts Fail', *Harvard Business Review*, March/April 1995: 59-67.

Mamic, I. (2003) 'Business and Codes of Conduct Implementation: How Firms Use Management Systems for Social Performance', ILO, Management and Corporate Citizenship Programme, www.ilo.org/images/empent/static/mcc/download/ supply_chain.pdf, accessed October 2004.

Mamic, I. (2004) *Implementing Codes of Conduct: How Businesses Manage Global Supply Chains* (Sheffield, UK: Greenleaf Publishing).

Margolis, J.D., and J.P. Walsh (2003) 'Misery Loves Companies: Rethinking Social Initiatives By Business', *Administrative Science Quarterly* 48: 268-305.

Muoio, A. (1990) 'Cisco's Quick Study', *Fast Company* 30 (October 2000): 286-90.

O'Reilly, C., and J. Pfeffer (2000) *Hidden Value: How Great Companies Achieve Extraordinary Results with Ordinary People* (Boston, MA: Harvard Business School Press).

Orlitzky, M., F.I. Schmidt and S.L. Rynes (2003) 'Corporate Social and Financial Performance: A Meta-Analysis', *Organization Studies* 24: 403-41.

Pfeffer, J. (1998) *The Human Equation: Building Profits by Putting People First* (Boston, MA: Harvard Business School Press).

—— and J.F. Veiga (1999) 'Putting People First for Organizational Success', *Academy of Management Executive* 13.2: 37-48.

Poirier, C.C., and W.F. Houser (1993) *Business Partnering for Continuous Improvement* (San Francisco: Berrett-Koehler).

Rochlin, S.A., and B. Christoffer (2000) *Making the Business Case: Determining the Value of Corporate Community Involvement* (Chestnut Hill, MA: Boston College Center for Corporate Community Relations).

Senge, P. (1990) *The Fifth Discipline: The Art and Practice of the Learning Organization* (New York: Free Press [rev. edn 2006]).

Strum, A., K. Müller and V.M. Panapanaan (2000) *Corporate Social Accountability Management: A Handbook on the Implementation of the New Standard on Corporate Social Accountability (SA8000)* (initiated by CEPAA; Washington, DC: Ellipson).

Van Heel, O.D., J. Elkington, S. Fennell and F. van Dijk (2001) *Buried Treasure: Uncovering the Business Case for Corporate Sustainability* (London: SustainAbility).

Waddock, S. (2006) *Leading Corporate Citizens: Vision, Values, Value Added* (New York: McGraw-Hill, 2nd edn).

—— and C. Bodwell (2002) 'From TQM to TRM: The Emerging Evolution of Total Responsibility Management (TRM) Systems', *Journal of Corporate Citizenship* 2.7 (Autumn 2002): 113-26.

—— and C. Bodwell (2004) 'Managing Responsibility: What Can Be Learned from the Quality Movement?', *California Management Review* 47.1 (Fall 2004): 25-37.

—— and S.B. Graves (1997a) 'Quality of Management and Quality of Stakeholder Relations: Are They Synonymous?', *Business and Society* 36.3 (September 1997): 250-79.

—— and S.B. Graves (1997b) The Corporate Social Performance–Financial Performance Link, *Strategic Management Journal* 18.4: 303-19.

—— and J. Leigh (2006) 'Voluntary Responsibility Management Systems in Global Supply Chains: The Emergence of Total Responsibility Management Approaches', *Business and Society Review* 111.4 (Winter 2006): 409-26.

—— and N. Smith (2000) 'Corporate Responsibility Audits: Doing Well by Doing Good', *Sloan Management Review* 41.2 (Winter 2000): 75-83.

—— C. Bodwell and S.B. Graves (2002) 'Responsibility: The New Business Imperative', *Academy of Management Executive* 16.2 (May 2002): 132-48.

Index